Walls

MURAL

WOOD PANEL

STENCIL

WALLPAPER

Florence de Dampierre

Principal photography by
Tim Street-Porter and Pieter Estersohn

RIZZOLI
NEW YORK

New York · Paris · London · Milan

contents

introduction

Painting is silent poetry,

and poetry painting that speaks.

—Plutarch, *De Gloria Atheniensum* (III, 346)

Throughout history, walls have provided endless opportunities to personalize spaces. More than a solid-colored backdrop blending in with furnishings and paintings, decorated walls create dramatic and subtle effects. As the author of the book *The Best of Painted Furniture*, I have developed, over the years, a great fondness for all sorts of painted surfaces. I especially find their beauty and sometimes whimsical nature extremely appealing. In my house and in many of my design projects, I have incorporated several types of wall treatments, ranging from wallpaper to faux finishes and wood paneling. These enhancements have had lasting effects. For this book I have chosen to examine four classic European and American wall treatments—mural, wood panel, stencil, and wallpaper—as they are not only historically important but also can transform today's interiors into stylish settings.

Decorated walls are a testament to our past, spanning prehistoric times to ancient Greco-Roman civilizations to the Renaissance and beyond. Beginning with the earthy, mysterious cave paintings, wall decorations have evolved to include elegant masterpieces. Reflecting both popular and cultivated tastes, this art has not only survived but flourished with well-documented works ranging from the allegorical to the realistic to simple design motifs.

Pompeii features some of the earliest examples of wall decoration in a domestic setting. It is chiefly through the hundreds of wall paintings discovered in the buried city that we have a full picture of Pompeian life. Throughout time, mural paintings have played a dual role as objects of beauty and educational vehicles. In churches they have conveyed biblical stories with a codified canon of figurative vignettes and symbols. Similarly, the popular French scenic wallpapers of the nineteenth century introduced people to foreign lands, exotic flora and fauna, and fashionable trends.

A fanciful chandelier and a painted hydrangea-blue faux molding embellish this serene, white bedroom. Interior designer John Barman decorated this New York City townhouse in the style of Christian Bérard.

Originally painted for the Cascina Bogino in Moncalieri, near Turin, this mural suite on canvas, c. 1810, was installed in the early twentieth-century antechamber of the Caramoor estate in Katonah, New York. The dreamy landscape and harbor scenes appear through the trompe l'oeil *pillars of a loggia.*

OVERLEAF, LEFT
A detail of an elaborate French-inspired nineteenth-century wallpaper from the Hacienda Jaral de Berrio in Mexico.

OVERLEAF, RIGHT
Eighteenth-century frescoes of Diana and her hunting party embellish the walls of the Ferragamo's dining room—a harmonious backdrop for the Murano glass chandelier, mahogany-and-walnut table, silk upholstered chairs, and the gilt-wood console.

More than mere decoration, wall treatments reflect the fashion and thinking of particular times. For example, the numerous Renaissance frescoes of the Palazzo del Te in Mantua illustrate the pageantry associated with the rulers of sixteenth-century Italy. The Duke of Mantua, Federico II Gonzaga, employed his court painter Giulio Romano (c. 1492–1546) to present him as a sensual warrior prince. The whimsical and dramatic frescoes throughout the palace reflect the duke's sentiments. One look at the erotic art of the *Sala di Psiche* or the *Sala dei Giganti*, laden with symbolic imagery such as Federico in the guise of Jupiter crushing giants, gives us an appreciation of the thinking of the time.

The Romans were fond of enchanted landscapes in which dreamy settings are filled with mythological iconography. Such wall imagery became popular many centuries later due to the writings of the French philosopher Jean-Jacques Rousseau and others—another example of techniques and themes which reoccur over time.

Throughout the centuries the cross-pollination brought about by East–West trade-inspired styles such as the exotic *chinoiserie* of a French Louis XIV pleasure pavilion or the Orientalism of the late nineteenth-century, exemplified by the Moorish marvels created for the homes of Frederic Edwin Church (1826–1900) and Louis Comfort Tiffany (1848–1933). The British architect and designer Robert Adam (1728–92) combined motifs in an attempt to infuse walls with the spirit of antiquity. He covered them with traceries, filigrees, and painted geometric Greek and Roman-inspired architectural ornaments, including urns and fans. Some artists, such as the itinerant painter Rufus Porter (1792–1884), who helped shape American culture, also mixed techniques. He painted murals of the developing nation's villages and landscapes, which he cleverly stenciled to speed up the decorating process.

This book explores how the classic techniques of wall decoration can be relevant in a modern setting. Guidelines to keep these decorative elements looking fresh are provided. I hope that these pages of glorious images, ranging from lavish coverings such as frescoes and *boiseries* to more affordable options like stenciling and wallpaper, will inspire and dazzle.

tapestries

Although I have not included a chapter devoted to wall hangings, tapestries in particular have played a role in the history of wall decoration and must be part of the conversation. These hangings serve as both insulation and decoration.

Hand-woven textiles primarily of silk or wool, tapestries have a long history as wall hangings, making their first appearance in ancient Babylonia and Assyria. These early examples, decorated with strange unicorns and griffins, have designs that reappeared in Eastern and Western art during the Middle Ages. Homer's epics, *The Iliad* and *The Odyssey*, refer to such tapestries, and records indicate that they played an important role in the decoration of Greek temples. In fact, the Parthenon's interior was draped with tapestries. During the reign of Alexander the Great, many were imported into Greece, where several centers devoted to the craft emerged. Not as active in their production, Rome imported tapestries from the East. Brighter colors were introduced by the Barbarian invasions; and the artisans of Gaul and Great Britain featured beautiful flora and fauna designs.

During Medieval times tapestries, embellished with expensive silver and gold thread, were more highly esteemed than paintings. Easily transported, they were ideal for insulating the large, drafty rooms of castles and churches or for display at tournaments. The rich and powerful commissioned them to fill up wall spaces or to fit into wood paneling with exact dimensions. The allegorical biblical representations often conveyed the glory of the owner. Between the tenth and thirteenth centuries, small workshops opened in the French towns of Poitiers and Limoges. Few tapestries from this time exist, but there are some fragments in London's Victoria and Albert Museum's collection.

In the beginning of the fourteenth century, a thriving tapestry industry emerged in the West, particularly in northern France and Flanders, in the towns of Paris and Arras, along with Brussels. Paris, with twenty-four master tapestry workers in 1292, had

Inspired by Tony Duquette, interior designer Peter Dunham created this tableau in his sitting room—a William IV painted-mahogany table against an eighteenth-century Florentine tapestry with trompe l'oeil architectural details in a subdued palette.

almost doubled that number by 1302. Begun in 1313, the Arras workshops produced many tapestries with chivalric, biblical, or mythological scenes. Few tapestries of this time are extant. Fortunately, the dramatic, large-scale tapestry *The Apocalypse*, with scenes from the book of Revelation, has survived and still graces the walls of the Château d'Angers.

Other centers such as Brussels were almost equal to Arras, which had declined by the mid-fifteenth century. Spanning almost the entire sixteenth century and into the seventeenth century, Brussels' tapestry factories produced many masterpieces, including those based on Raphael's famous *Acts of the Apostles* cartoons of 1515–16 (in the Victoria and Albert Museum) for the Sistine Chapel. In the late fifteenth and sixteenth centuries, the talented Flemish painter Bernard van Orley (1487–1541) established himself as a leading painter of cartoons for the

The Arcadia tapestry is artist Thomas McKnight's contemporary interpretations of the myths of Apollo and Daphne (on the right) and Paris and Artemis.

weavers. His well-known tapestry series *The Hunts of Maximilian* of 1525–40 (in the Louvre) and the *Battle of Pavia* woven for Charles V in 1531 (in the Museo di Capodimonte, Naples) initiated the custom of commemorating the deeds of rulers. Empty space was left, usually in the middle of the top border, for the coat of arms or cipher of the purchaser. Though their output was smaller than Brussels' was, the French began a royal industry at Fontainebleau. The subsequent French kings Henry II and Henry IV admired the craft, ordering tapestries for their châteaux. During Louis XIV's reign, the Manufactures des Gobelins and later Aubusson created spectacular tapestries. The quality of craftsmanship of tapestries has endured to this day with leading twentieth-century artists including Fernand Léger and Raoul Dufy; even contemporary artists such as the American Thomas McKnight have created designs for their looms.

A stylized depiction of lilies of the valley is seen in this dreamy landscape. The classic tonality of this detail of the Arcadia tapestry, produced in Aubusson, France, in 1991, is reminiscent of ancient frescoes.

mural

Since prehistoric times, human beings have adorned their shelters as well as communal and spiritual places with meaningful imagery. One of the oldest forms of wall decoration, murals are works of art painted directly on walls, ceilings, or other permanent surfaces. The function of murals varies from culture to culture; they can be allegories, records of events, or even social or political statements. The first murals we know of are cave paintings from the Paleolithic Age. Vestiges have been found at Altamira in northern Spain and at Lascaux and the Grotte de Pech-Merle in France's Lot region.

A wide variety of artistic styles and techniques have been used to portray complex scenes that are visible up close and far away. Recent excavations of early settlements in Turkey, dating from 7,000 to 5,500 B.C., reveal fresco as one of the earliest mural techniques. With the advent of oil paint in the fifteenth century, painted murals evolved in a variety of ways. Often backed with canvas, murals ranged from figurative to *trompe l'oeil* in style.

Artisans in ancient Egypt and the Near East painted murals on the ceilings and walls of royal tombs, temples, and palaces. Egyptians painted mural scenes depicting secular events in the life of the Pharaoh and themes of religious significance. These Egyptian paintings portrayed the wonders of the natural world in a sensitive manner. Not much painted decoration has survived from Mesopotamia. What have been found are bold, geometric designs, occasionally combined with representations of human figures and other naturalistic forms, which embellished the elaborate interiors of Babylonia and Assyria.

Decorating wall surfaces with fresco paintings gained prominence during the Roman, Byzantine, Romanesque, and Renaissance periods. Glorious imagery from ancient times can still be seen at Herculaneum and Pompeii. Pompeian frescoes, which exemplify the zenith of fresco technique, are characterized by an innate perfection of form and outline as well as by subtle restraint. For the most part, artists chose a subdued range of tints rather than more vivid hues. In fact "Pompeian red" remains a favorite color today and is still one of the most effective tones for mural backgrounds. Painted to last, Pompeian walls are time capsules. Two thousand years have not diminished their grandeur. The stable pigments employed remain so fresh and so unfaded that the colors bounce to life. One would swear those lively frescoes of nymphs and satyrs and gods and goddesses were painted yesterday. Their extraordinary durability is due to a careful preparation of gum arabic with melted wax and a special kind of skillfully applied varnish-oil.

The Middle Ages and the Renaissance

The murals of the French and Italian churches and monasteries from the Middle Ages followed a strict code, drawing on the writings of Grégoire de Tours and Sidoine Apollinaire. Serving the Catholic Church as a form of instruction, they showed the pleasures of heaven, the miseries of hell, and Adam and Eve expelled from paradise. These frequently depicted parables became known as the *Biblia pauperum* (the poor person's bible) because they presented biblical stories in a clear, visual narrative to a largely illiterate population.

Frescoes peaked in Italy during the Renaissance with masters such as Giotto (1267–1337), Raphael (1483–1520), and Michelangelo (1475–1564). Apart from their functional didactic value, frescoes tested the skills of the finest artists, including Giotto, Masaccio (1401–28), and Michelangelo. They told stories on the walls about the saint to whom the church was dedicated, the religious order, or the patron families of the chapels.

Historically valuable as picture postcards from the past, frescoes show images of daily life—for example, cityscapes with buildings, furnishings, and people dressed in the attire of the time. In Ghirlandaio's frescoes (1485–90) at the Tornabuoni Chapel in the Florentine church Santa Maria Novella, one can admire the fine clothes of noblewomen and the interiors of luxurious fifteenth-century villas.

The Fresco Technique

In the elaborate process of fresco painting, pigments are applied to a freshly plastered ground. Extremely time-sensitive, this technique requires not just artistic ability but also a physical finesse for adding decoration before the plaster has set.

OPPOSITE

Displaying the world as it was known during the late sixteenth century, this fresco painted by Antonio Giovanni de Varese in 1574 graces the interior of the Sala del Mappamondo *(Hall of the World Maps) in the Villa Farnese, Caprarola, Italy. The ceiling vaults have painted depictions of the celestial spheres and the constellation of the zodiac.*

OVERLEAF, LEFT

Seventeenth-century frescoes decorate the vaults of Teodoli Castle's arched veranda on the outskirts of Rome. The walls below are painted in grisaille with gold swags.

OVERLEAF, RIGHT

The loggia of the Roman Palazzo Altemps has a vaulted arcade decorated with frescoes. Now a museum, it houses the Ludovisi collection of ancient Roman sculptures.

In fact, "fresco" is derived from the Italian word "*affresco*," which means fresh. To make tempera paint, natural-colored pigments extracted from minerals are ground and mixed with water and tempered with size (a semi-solid glutinous substance). Size was often replaced by egg yolk as an adhesive. Gum, honey, or milk of a fig tree can also be used as a binder. For "true" fresco, the tempera is applied to a thin coat of plaster (or gesso) on the surface while it is still wet. The colors become lighter when dry. Careful layering of light tones over dark creates a beautiful opalescence. An easier method, known as *fresco secco*, is to apply pigments with a glue or casein base on a dry plaster surface.

The Tempera Tradition

ABOVE

*The frescoes of the late
eighteenth-century garden
pavilion of Villa Giulia
in Palermo were designed
for public enjoyment.
The dominant color is
Pompeian red.*

OPPOSITE

*The Villa Torrigiani, a
rococo-style private home
outside of Lucca, was
completely modified by
Marchese Nicolao Santini,
ambassador to the Court of
Louis XIV, in the seventeenth
century. The frescoes in
the loggia create an almost
cinematic illusion.*

The use of tempera for wall murals and paneling continued in Western Europe during the Romanesque period, achieving prominence in Italy. Until the time of Raphael in the sixteenth century, artists of the Italian School produced amazing feats of technical virtuosity with frescoes. Cennino d'Andrea Cennini, a Florentine artist of the Renaissance (born in 1370), wrote a treatise on the subject in 1437, *Il Libro dell' Arte* or *Il Trattato della Pittura*, which includes all the recipes for painting during his day. In a highly detailed description of egg and tempera, he advised using the white of the egg particularly for gilding, but for painting he recommended egg yolk. Eggs had to be fresh, and both country and town eggs needed to be available. Country eggs were redder and better suited to making the color blue. Town eggs were whiter and thus appropriate for lighter colors. He suggested painting young faces with town eggs, while country eggs were preferable for painting old men.

Cennino also explained the techniques of the Giottesque school. Giotto, one of the first great artists to contribute to the Italian Renaissance, painted spectacular

frescoes. This Florentine artist's first masterpiece, the frescoes in the Arena Chapel at Padua, is a milestone in Western painting. A starry sky covers the vaulted ceiling. The central mural in the nave depicts Christ and Mary, framed by *The Last Judgment* and *The Annunciation* witnessed by God. In between, the story of Mary is narrated on the upper register of the walls, and the early years of Jesus with the story of his Passion are narrated on the two lower registers. Giotto and his assistants painted from top to bottom. Since the painting was executed *affresco*, moist plaster had to be applied only to the surface that could be decorated in one day. Without helpers, it would have been impossible to realize such a monumental program in the short span of two to three years.

High Renaissance Frescoes and Murals

Important political or spiritual figures of the time often employed artists to create major wall and ceiling decorations to celebrate their lives. Commissioned in 1459 and painted by Benozzo Gozzoli (1420–97), *The Procession of the Magi*, which covers the walls of the chapel in the Medici-Riccardi Palace in Florence, features the great art patron Lorenzo de' Medici. Demonstrating his superior equestrian mastery,

27

Lorenzo sits imperially on his trotting white horse. He wears Florentine red like the others in his retinue, and the horses are brilliantly turned out in *caparisons* (decorative trappings) of red and gold or blue and yellow. Such frescoes visually recorded the lives of the nobility. Ferdinando de' Medici continued the family tradition of commissioning fashionable artists to create magnificent frescoes for his *studiolo* (study or library) in the Villa Medici in Rome. For the antechamber, Nanni di Baccio Bigio and Bartolomeo Ammannati painted a colorful variety of bird species in a garden pergola.

Raphael began spectacular frescoes in 1508 for the Vatican apartment of Pope Julius II. He introduced portraits of his contemporaries in the most masterly of them, the epic *School of Athens*. The composition's focal point, the two philosophers Plato and Aristotle, stand at the top of the steps. One of Raphael's apprentices in Rome, Giulio Romano, an Italian painter and architect, became his principle heir and artistic executor, completing several of the artist's Vatican frescoes. Romano lived from 1524 in Mantua, where he developed a personal, anti-classical style and came to dominate the artistic activity at the Gonzaga court. His most important commissioned fresco, in the Palazzo del Te, was begun in 1526, and is a tour de force. The *Sala dei Giganti* is one of the most sensational creations of this palace, borrowing the myth of the Giants from Ovid's *Metamorphoses*. His illusionistic painting prefigured the baroque period.

Another fresco master is Michelangelo, known to his contemporaries as *Il Terribile*. Rejecting all the assumptions of the Renaissance, he revolutionized all he touched, and his style, an intermingling of sweetness and strength, is unique in the history of art. His greatest accomplishment is the ceiling fresco of the Sistine Chapel, originally built for Pope Sixtus IV. This simple brick structure's height is sixty-eight feet, with a shallow barrel vault flattened at the top. On this surface, Michelangelo created his masterpiece.

Other wall curiosities of the middle of the sixteenth century are grotesques, a decorative genre inspired by Nero's *Domus Aurea* (Latin for "Golden House"). Revived in Rome due to the fascination of Raphael's circle with archaeological discoveries, grotesques were popular with the Florentine School of decoration and involved a fantastic interlacing of forms: plants with human figures, cupids, real and fanciful animals, curling tendrils, and other swirling images. Painter and art historian Giorgio Vasari in his book *Lives of the Most Eminent Painters, Sculptors, and Architects* of 1550 described them as "a kind of free and humorous picture produced by the ancients for the decoration of vacant spaces in some position

OPPOSITE
The remarkable frescoes of the Palazzo del Te, built near Mantua between 1526 and 1534, follow iconographic themes: love and the accomplishments of Federico II Gonzaga. This detail from the spectacular Sala dei Giganti, *takes inspiration from the first book of Ovid's* Metamorphoses. *Giulio Romano's masterpiece is a perfect example of mannerism, with its mixture of reality and fantasy and the grotesque, with a sense of humor.*

OVERLEAF, LEFT
Grotesques, winged animals, griffins, and medallions adorn the small living room's frescoed walls, dating from the eighteenth century, in the Ferragamo's carefully restored Tuscan villa. An antique sofa and armchairs complete the room.

OVERLEAF, RIGHT
Whimsical Pompeian-style arabesques permeate this villa to include even the bathroom frescoes. The large tub is Portoro marble.

where only things placed high are suitable. For this purpose they fashioned monsters deformed by a freak of nature or by the whim or fancy of the workers . . ." Beautiful grotesques can be admired at the Villa Antinori delle Rose on the outskirts of Florence. In this breathtaking house, a small living room is adorned with grotesques, winged animals, griffins, and medallions.

The Introduction of Oil Painting

The introduction of oil-based paints occurred during the fifteenth century in Flanders. Used by such masters as Jan van Eyck (died 1441) and Rogier van der Weyden (1399–1464), tempera painting gradually lost its prominence as the medium for making major works of art and was superseded by oil painting. Vasari, in *Lives of the Most Eminent Painters, Sculptors, and Architects*, said that oil painting was "a most beautiful invention and a great convenience to the art of painting." The most well-known application of oil paint before the end of the fifteenth century is Leonardo da Vinci's *Last Supper* in Milan. However, experts have discovered that Leonardo did not use pure oil paint. A spectral image of the masterpiece shows that very little of his handiwork has survived. In fact, at that time, tempera was favored for large wall decorations. Some artists, such as Andrea Mantegna (1431–1506), not only produced wall murals but painted canvases as well. His beautiful frescoes grace the Church of S. Giustina in Padua (1448–55), yet he painted on canvas his great work, now at Hampton Court in England, *The Triumph of Caesar*. Legendary artists such as the Venetian Giambattista Tiepolo (1696–1770), renowned for his fresco decorations, and the Spaniard Francisco Goya (1746–1828), who painted frescoes in the cupola of S. Antonio de la Florida in Madrid in 1798, used the tempera medium. We learn through Vasari's writings that the Venetians introduced mural painting on canvas in the fifteenth century because the climate was unsuitable for the preservation of frescoes.

During the Italian Renaissance, some artists painted murals on canvas with oil-based paint. This enabled the murals to travel safely throughout the Continent, spreading the riches of different cultures. Canvas construction developed, including a technique called *marouflage* for adhering a painted canvas to a wall in order to create a mural. This was accomplished by coating the surface with white lead mixed with oil. The Italian influence spread quickly in France, especially under King François I (1494–1547). He invited talented Italian artists to work at Fontainebleau, his favorite residence, where he wanted to build a palace worthy of royalty. He commissioned Italian painters capable of producing large wall decorations, including

From the frescoes to the coffered ceiling, the Sala della Fontana, *a reception room in the Roman Palazzo Colonna, is a golden Arcadian masterpiece. The fifteenth-century ceiling frescoes are by Pinturicchio; the wall murals echo the vistas outside.*

the master Leonardo da Vinci. Artists Rosso Fiorentino (1495–1540) of Florence and Francesco Primaticcio (1504–79) of Bologna imported the method of painting large fresco murals with architectural decorations. Primaticcio had worked with Giuolo Romano on the Palazzo del Te in Mantua. For the king's gallery, he produced a series of thirteen allegorical and mythological paintings on wood panel, which are surrounded with stucco decoration. This extraordinary ensemble is considered to be the first example of décor "à la française."

Wall Murals of the Baroque Period

During the seventeenth century's baroque period, panel painting on canvas became more fashionable than fresco. The most prolific artist was the Flemish Peter Paul Rubens (1577–1640), who painted a series of murals from 1622 to 1625 for Marie

de Medici in the Luxembourg Palace. All twenty-four paintings are in the Louvre. Rubens also decorated Jesuit churches in Antwerp and the banqueting hall of Whitehall in London.

The seventeenth century was also a seminal period in the development of French decorative art, particularly during the reign of King Louis XIV. Charles Le Brun (1619–90) became the all-powerful artistic master in France. Trained as a painter under Simon Vouet, he studied in Rome and acquired from Nicolas Poussin and Pietro da Cortona a classic high baroque style. Le Brun created the interior decorations and wall painting at the Château de Vaux le Vicomte in 1661. Engaged in royal service shortly after, Le Brun and his team of craftsmen painted their first major wall decoration for the king—the *Galerie d'Apollo* at the Château du Louvre. Depicting scenes from the life of Alexander, these murals so entranced the king that their completion instantly earned Le Brun a place among the nobility as well as the title *Premier Peintre du Roi* (First Painter to His Majesty). In 1667, he decorated many rooms in the new Château de Saint Germain and decorated Versailles, specifically the grand staircase, the *Galerie des Glaces* (Hall of Mirrors), and the *Salons de la Guerre et de la Paix* (Salons of War and Peace).

Chinoiserie and Singerie

In the late seventeenth century, *chinoiserie*, with a new range of imagery, emerged as a result of the West's fascination with the Far East. The French court of Versailles re-imagined this exotic style and made it fashionable. Indeed, the legendary Sun King built a small pleasure house influenced by Chinese architecture *Pavilion de Porcelaine,* for his favorite mistress, Madame de Montespan. This fantasy structure not only led to the many exquisite architectural curiosities that adorn many European parks—from Drottningholm and Palermo to Sintra and Tsarkoe-Selo—but also inspired spectacular *chinoiserie* wallpapers, lacquered surfaces, and painted murals. Walls became populated with strange and witty little animals, pagodas, and ladies strolling with fanciful parasols. The perfect vehicle for evoking the mysteries of this faraway land—the Chinese monkey—was particularly appealing with its bizarre look.

Singerie (the French word for "monkey decoration") emerged during the eighteenth-century as a new decorative style incorporating monkey imagery. In his engravings, the French artist Jean Bérain the Elder (1638–1711) replaced classical fauns with monkeys, cleverly adapted Raphaelesque grotesque ornaments to the current taste, and also used arabesque designs. In 1709 another Frenchman,

Built in 1753, the Chinese Pavilion on the grounds of the Drottningholm Palace, exemplifies the widespread popularity of chinoiserie *decoration.*

36

the artist Claude Audran III (1658–1734), painted an arbor with monkeys seated at a table for the walls of the Château de Marly. The *singerie* style was born. Jean-Antoine Watteau (1684–1721), who had trained under Audran at Marly, later painted *Les Singes Peintres* for the Regent as a pendant to Pieter Brueghel the Elder's *La Musique des Chats*. The spirit of fantasy in Watteau's *chinoiseries* was pushed further by Christophe Huet (1700–1759) in mural paintings on canvas inserted in wood panels, known as *La Grande Singerie*, for several of the rooms at the Château de Chantilly in 1735. One of the most whimsical surviving examples of French rococo interior decoration, the main figures are chinamen with their monkey attendants, amiable little animals capering over the walls and ceilings. The

38

naughty little creatures revolt against the stifling constraints of the baroque period by clambering about the château's walls and conversing with each other dressed in flowing Mandarin gowns or the garb of nobility.

In nineteenth-century England, the Prince Regent (who later became King George IV), for whom the Regency style is named, promoted the *chinoiserie* decorative style too. His palace in Brighton, England, was redesigned by John Nash from 1815 to 1822. Known as the Royal Pavilion, it was filled with *chinoiserie*, Indian treasures, and other exotic hand-painted decoration, including stenciling. This fashionable trend was so popular throughout the Continent that palaces continued to be constructed in the *chinoiserie* style.

ABOVE AND LEFT

*Linen and silk were
elegant alternatives
to canvas. Installed in
the powder room at
Caramoor in New York, this
nineteenth-century hand-
painted linen mural is a
Western interpretation of
Chinese life.*

OPPOSITE

*By the end of the
seventeenth century in
Europe, monkeys were
associated with China.
It is possible that this
imagery was first imported
through Chinese porcelains
and then used for decorative
schemes. In this chinoiserie
painting on silk, the
mischievous monkey and
other fantastical four-
legged beasts inhabit the
tree peonies. It is mounted
on panels in the Monkey
Bedroom at Caramoor.*

The chinoiserie details in the Ferragamos' bedroom were inspired by the restored original Eastern-style frescoes. They form a backdrop for an eighteenth-century bench covered in antique silk and Florentine armchairs.

This nineteenth-century aquatint depicts the interior of the Royal Pavilion's banqueting room at Brighton Palace by John Nash (1752–1835). The fanciful interior design, primarily by Frederick Crace and Robert Jones, incorporates both Indian and Chinese decorative motifs. Private collection.

This exotic villa of King Ferdinando I of the Two Sicilies in Palermo was designed by Marvuglia in 1799. It is an example of Chinese-revival architectural and decorative style, mixed with neoclassical elements, which was popular throughout Europe from England to Russia.

The Rococo Style

The rococo period of the eighteenth century was a natural evolution from the florid bravura of the baroque. The signature motifs are ornate, playful, and lighthearted. Jean-Honoré Fragonard (1732–1806), François Boucher (1703–70), Jean-Antoine Watteau, and Giambattista Tiepolo were the prominent artists. In France, Boucher's work epitomized the sensuous hedonism and gaiety of mid-eighteenth century courtly life. His style influenced decorative arts throughout Europe. Boucher demonstrated his splendid technique in the *Salon de Gille Demarteau* with inset mural paintings of mythological animals in a playful setting (now the Musée Carnavalet in Paris).

The Italian tradition of fresco decoration begun by Giotto four hundred years earlier was mastered during the eighteenth century by the prolific Italian painter Tiepolo. The artist shared with his great Veronese predecessor a love of pageantry and sparkling color, often portraying sixteenth-century costumes in his paintings. But during the mid-1720s, he preferred fresco because of its lighter palette. Tiepolo created exhilarating effects of airy space, particularly with his ceiling frescoes, in which the central area are often depictions of open sky.

44

These charming pastoral scenes and harbor views, painted in tempera on paper, are in La Loggia bedroom at Caramoor. Originally made in the eighteenth century for the Villa La Loggia near Turin, Italy, the young lady on the swing is reminiscent of rococo master Jean-Honoré Fragonard's famous risqué painting The Swing of 1767.

In each country the rococo style had a national character, and there were many local variants as well. In England, wall painting was less predominant. German and Austrian mural painters merged the still vigorous Baroque tradition with the confectionary rococo style. Daniel Gran (1694–1757) and Paul Troger (1698–1762), Viennese mural painters, created light-filled, exuberant masterpieces. The Austrian decorative painter Franz Anton Maulbertsch (1724–96) created colorful and emotional painted church altarpieces as well as mural paintings and frescoes for buildings throughout the Austro-Hungarian Empire.

The Neoclassic, Romantic, and Other Painted Mural Styles

By the mid-eighteenth century, the frivolity of the rococo style was replaced by neoclassicism. Archaeological discoveries of the frescoes at Pompeii and Herculaneum prompted a return to classical iconography. Greek, Roman, and Italian Renaissance art inspired numerous neoclassical wall decorations and murals. Josephine de Beauharnais's dining room at Malmaison, designed by the neoclassical architectural duo Charles Percier (1764–1838) and Pierre-François Léonard Fontaine (1762–1853) is decorated with a series of Pompeian-style dancers painted on stucco by Louis Lafitte. Neoclassicism gave way in the nineteenth century to romanticism. Eugène Delacroix's (1798–1863) dramatic and colorful murals for Paris's Church of Saint Sulpice (1856–61) and the Château du Louvre (1859–61) are stellar examples.

Other artistic movements include the German Romantic Nazarenes, as well as the English Pre-Raphaelites, both of whom resurrected the medieval tradition of painted murals. They sought to return to art that embodied the spiritual values associated with the late Middle Ages and the Renaissance. Mural painting saw a renaissance. Between 1857 and 1859, the Pre-Raphaelites painted murals in the Old Library at the Oxford Union in Oxford, England. Dante Gabriel Rossetti (1828–82) oversaw the creation of tempera murals depicting scenes from the Arthurian legends on the walls of the Oxford Union Society's Debating Hall painted by the Pre-Raphaelite brotherhood. Sadly, the walls were not properly prepared, so the brilliantly colored works dissolved almost immediately. William Morris (1834–96) learned from this unfortunate mistake and subsequently paid close attention to the quality of materials he used for his later creative endeavors. Morris's Red House in the south of London is an artistic jewel created by leading members of his fellow Pre-Raphaelites. Murals include Edward Burne-Jones's scenes painted

For the boudoir of Marie-Antoinette (1755–93) in the Château de Fontainebleau, Seine-et-Marne, France, the artist Richard Mique (1728–94) painted this neoclassical-style panel mural, c. 1786, framed with elegant painted wood paneling. It is one of the most beautiful examples of eighteenth-century wall decoration.

49

ABOVE
These wall decorations (1803–10) in Paris's Hotel de Beauharnais's Salon de Musique feature painted panels with Pompeian overtones, and depict the seasons, muses, and musical attributes.

BELOW
The decorative scheme of the Pompeian room at Ickworth House, England, was designed by John Diblee Crace (1838–1919) in 1879. These oil-on-canvas wall paintings, are based on Roman frescoes, including a graceful depiction of a nymph with a bucket.

OPPOSITE
During the late eighteenth century, the king of Sweden Gustav III created a neoclassical-style pavilion in Haga Park. The decorative multi-paneled wall scheme is embellished with medallions and friezes depicting Greek mythological scenes set in lustrous frames.

OVERLEAF, LEFT
This Federal-style fresco in Washington, Connecticut's historic Red House includes both symbolic and mythological imagery, and a 1782 version of America's Great Seal.

OVERLEAF, RIGHT
This flower-filled urn in Rancho de la Capilla, Mexico, embodies details typical of sixteenth- and seventeenth-century Mexican design.

This exquisite watercolor drawing (1896–97) of a design for the mural decoration of Miss Cranston's Buchanan Street Tearooms, in Glasgow, is by the Scottish architect and designer, Charles Rennie Mackintosh. He was a leading proponent of the arts and crafts and art nouveau movements in Great Britain. Glasgow University Art Gallery, Scotland.

in tempera depicting the wedding of Sir Degravant. The fashion for murals continued during the art nouveau period. Scottish architect Charles Rennie Mackintosh's (1868–1928) floral design for the mural decoration of Miss Cranston's Buchanan Street Tearooms (1896–97) in Glasgow epitomizes this style.

The Popularity of Mural Painting in Public Spaces

With the advent of world's fairs, murals became the vehicle for expressing social or political issues on a grand scale with maximum impact. Mary Cassatt and Kenyon Cox created masterful murals for the 1890's Chicago World's Fair. The 1931 Exposition Coloniale in Paris featured spectacular art deco frescoes paired with modernist furniture by Emile-Jacques Ruhlmann (1879–1933).

Large public spaces, such as libraries and government buildings, became the new venue for murals. Celebrated examples include Pierre Puvis de Chavannes's murals entitled *Pastoral Poetry* of 1895 to 1898 and John Singer Sargent's large-scale murals depicting the history of religion, both of which grace the walls of the Boston Public Library. The prominent Mexican painter Diego Rivera (1886–1957) also embraced the mural for political purposes when he painted remarkable frescoes in Mexico City depicting his country's 1910 revolution. His compatriots José Clemente Orozco (1883–1949) and Rufino Tamayo (1899–1991) joined in, also creating revolutionary murals.

Leading artists of the twentieth century were commissioned to create murals for civic projects. For example, Pablo Picasso painted the *Fall of Icarus* in the

UNESCO building in Paris; Henri Matisse decorated the chapel at St. Paul de Vence in Provence; Marc Chagall painted wall murals for Paris's Opera House and Lincoln Center in New York. Others such as Joan Miró created spectacular public murals.

Twentieth-Century Mural Paintings in a Domestic Setting

Mural decorations in public spaces reemerged in the twentieth century and continue today. Many serve political or commercial purposes. Simultaneously, murals have again become popular for the home. These works of art can have more dramatic impact than a painting due to their size and prominence. Some contemporary artists have been inspired by the pastoral genre of the French rococo to create a dreamy ambience but, instead, have chosen a neutral palette to imbue their work with a contemporary spin. Leading artists such as Sol LeWitt and Jonathan Borofsky have employed their signature abstract motifs in murals. A transforming decorative statement, murals should be well executed and appropriately placed.

This color lithograph, published in 1847, of the Imereth frescoes from the Gelati Monastery, depicts Russian royalty. The included text is by Count Ernest Stackelbert. Private Collection.

Built as the office of Maréchal Lyautey and decorated by Eugene Printz, this muraled room with stylized scenes of African culture by Bouquet was exhibited in the 1931 Exposition Coloniale in Paris. The facing room with more exotic Bouquet scenes contrasts wonderfully with the modernist lines of the Emile-Jacques Ruhlmann chair. Both spaces are now in the Musée de l'Afrique et d'Oceanie, Paris.

ABOVE

This delightful panoramic mural in a New York City dining room was painted by Nadia Wolinski.

BELOW

Another dining room mural features sea grass on the water's edge below a calming vista.

OPPOSITE

Decorator Thomas Beeton brought in Scott Flack to work on a Lois Esformes–designed bathroom for a house in Pacific Palisades, California. The mural depicting an Arcadian Eden by Flack is set in a neoclassical niche surrounded by an old-fashioned bateau bath.

OVERLEAF, ABOVE LEFT

Le Corbusier painted several frescoes with polymorphic shapes during the mid-twentieth century; this one in his friends' simple Amagansett, Long Island, farmhouse.

OVERLEAF, BELOW LEFT AND RIGHT

In Argentina the Estancias Los Alamos boasts several captivating mural paintings. The ranches' sprightly bedroom mural depicts a horse-drawn carriage, while the study's mural has a golden palette to complement the wood.

MURAL ESSENTIALS

FRESCOES

Since antiquity, frescoes have been painted in tempera, a pigment with an egg-yolk base. Similar to contemporary acrylic paint, tempera is not prone to cracking or yellowing like oil paint. Those unfamiliar with tempera often assume incorrectly that the bright yellow color of the egg yolk interferes with the look of the paint. When tempera dries, it loses the intensity of the yellow almost immediately. The beauty of tempera is that it enables the full brilliance of pigments to show through.

COLOR TIPS

Painting light tones over dark results in a translucent effect. If mixing is done properly, the colors won't rub off yet will remain water-soluble. For "true" fresco, the lime of the plaster functions as the binder. When dried, it forms calcium carbonate that incorporates the pure pigments, which are ground and diluted with water. The tone becomes brighter upon drying, and this color shift should be taken into consideration especially with deep tones. The distinctive opaque quality is produced by a medium that permits the layering of colors, one upon another.

OIL-PAINTED MURALS ON CANVAS

A painted mural seems like a daunting project. However, it can look breathtaking in a dining room or spacious hallway. If you turn to a professional mural painter, he or she is trained to layer the colors to achieve a desired effect. Today paint choices range from oil to latex. You can have a mural painted on a canvas surface and mounted to the wall or painted directly on the wall.

CARE AND MAINTENANCE

- The canvas used for a mural is pliable so putting pressure on the front or back surfaces could cause a dent or a hole. If such an accident occurs, consult an expert to repair the damage.
- Make sure a room with a mural does not have extreme temperature fluctuations or harsh sunlight.
- To protect a mural on canvas when temporarily storing or transporting it, place cardboard or plywood on both the front and the back, slightly larger than its outside dimensions. Cover the work in bubble wrap. Avoid storing it in a basement or attic.
- To help preserve a mural that is relatively new and doesn't have a relief surface in danger of being dislodged, gentle, light cleaning is recommended. At the time of purchase, obtain advice on maintenance because each mural has a specific set of variables.
- For fragile, old, or contemporary murals, especially those with cracks or fissures on the painted surface, consult a professional restorer. Dirt can accumulate. Those with a varnished protective surface can yellow.

LEFT: A detail of a landscape mural in a subdued green palette by Nadia Wolinski graces a Litchfield County living room that I designed. OPPOSITE: The living room mantelpiece in my former New York City townhouse is embellished with a playful mural of a lighthearted rendition of neoclassical motifs.

wood panel

D ue to its natural beauty, wood paneling has enhanced wall surfaces for many centuries. Wood is not only a versatile material but it is also plentiful throughout the world. Wood paneling ranges from the basic—plain wood planks, wainscoting, and beadboard—to elaborate *intarsia* (wood-inlay) and *boiserie*. In all forms, it creates a warm and inviting ambience that can be understated or dramatic. Plain and elaborately carved panels have dressed up walls and covered ceilings, sometimes with painted canvases between the panels. Paneled rooms have been inset with mirrors, rare woods, porcelain, or stones; others have been painted *en grisaille*, in *trompe l'oeil*, or to imitate rare wood or marble. Some incorporate images from the Bible or depict the Tree of Life, while others are adorned with *chinoiserie* decorations. Wood panels have also been completely lacquered, with different finishes such as *vernis martin* and *lacca contraffatta*. The look depends on the region, period, personal style, and how it fits into the overall design scheme. Ambitious undertakings, as with certain palaces of the past, required a high level of craftsmanship. Today, it can be quite costly to pay for skilled craftsmen, but it can produce paneling of lasting value.

The Middle Ages

Since the Middle Ages, wood paneling has been used as a finish for the interiors of churches and castles. Serving the dual purpose of design and comfort, it provided thermal insulation at the bottom of walls, which were often made of stone. Warmth was a prime consideration, and some solutions included paneling to chair-rail height with tapestries hung above. Though more costly, paneling was also installed up to the top of the ceiling; to keep more heat in, the ceiling was covered with paneling as well. Elaborately carved wood panels

Trompe l'oeil *pilasters and shadowy landscapes grace the entrance walls of the palatial stone mansion Sandemar Manor in Sweden, c. 1680, while the ceiling under the stairs is decorated in grisaille.*

enhanced medieval great halls. Penhurst Place (1340 A.D.) in Kent, England, offers a beautiful example of the Gothic style—panels adorned by perpendicular tracery with ogees and trefoils topped by crenellations. This style of woodcarving decoration is found in church steeples, choir stalls, and cloisterlike arcades of this period.

The church emerged as a major power in the Middle Ages, and religious ceremonies were an important part of everyday life, requiring the grandest possible settings. Carved and painted wood paneling were essential to display this considerable wealth and power. As the Gothic style gave way to the Renaissance, wood paneling evolved as well. The technique of inlay and marquetry developed as the guilds trained more artisans in woodcraft. Demand for their skills increased. Extraordinary woodwork was showcased in the Cabinet of Curiosities (also known as the Cabinet of Wonders), an elaborately designed room for the display of collections of religious and historic relics, works of art, antiquities, and marvels from the natural world.

The Renaissance Studiolo:
An Elaborate Library

Renaissance Italy introduced *intarsia*, a new type of wood-inlay paneling. With *intarsia* varied sizes of different woods create a mosaiclike design. The masterful Italian painters Paolo Uccello and Piero della Francesca designed *intarsia* panels. This technique belongs to the same family as inlay and later marquetry or parquetry. *Intarsia* designs consisted of geometric shapes until about 1450, at which time representational motifs began to appear. Architectural perspective drawings mixed with rare music or scientific instruments became popular, especially for the walls of the *studiolo*, a small study retreat. Dukes and popes wanted their *studiolos* decorated with sophisticated wood paneling. Federico de Montefeltro, tenth count of Urbino (1422–82), an admired military leader and humanist as well as famous for his vast knowledge of math, architecture, and the arts, created a great palace in the Renaissance style and hired the Sienese painter, sculptor, and engineer Francesco di Giorgio Martini to design the refined interior. His Urbino palace has a celebrated *studiolo* of about 1480, which can still be admired today. Conceived as a tiny chamber totally enclosed by continuous wooden illusionistic wainscoting executed in Florence with *intarsia* inlay, the Urbino *studiolo* became known as one of the marvels of the ducal palace. The *studiolo*'s success encouraged the duke to plan another extraordinary wood-paneled study for his palace at Gubbio. (This *studiolo* is now in the collection of the Metropolitan Museum of Art, New York City.) The complex design was created through latticework for the cabinet doors, decorative borders, and the Florentine technique of "perspective" *intarsia*.

Demonstrating the importance and popularity of wood paneling in the overall design scheme, it is interesting to note that Pope Leo X was so pleased with Raphael's fresco work in St. Peter's Basilica that he wanted to make sure that the paneling was worthy of the paintings. He sent an envoy to Monte Oliveto in Chiusuri to commission Fra Giovanni da Verona, a master of perspective views in wood inlay. Fra Giovanni executed not only the surrounding paneling but also fine doors and chairs, which won him generous praise and rewards from the pope. Expensive *studiolos* became a status symbol, as was Francesco I de Medici's, a wood-paneled room designed in the 1570s by Giorgio Vasari. Its walls and ceiling are covered with paintings. The fashion for *studiolos* continued in France during the sixteenth century. Writer Honoré de Balzac described the *Cabinet des Secrets* of Queen Catherine de Medici (1519–89) in the Château de Blois in his book *Catherine de Medici*: "In

Elegant intarsia
*paneling lines the Duke
of Urbino's study in the
Palazzo Ducale with
inventive* trompe l'oeil
*wood designs by Baccio
Pontelli (d. 1492).
These details depict
a reading stand and
a cupboard with a
latticework door,
revealing Pontelli's
extraordinary
craftsmanship. It is
one of the most
important examples of
the lost art of* intarsia.

this cabinet an observer will still find traces of that taste for gilding which Catherine brought with her from Italy . . ." for the princesses of her house "loved to veneer the castles of France with the gold earned by their ancestors in commerce, and to hang out their wealth on the walls of their apartments."

During the fifteenth and sixteenth centuries, the fashion for *intarsia* spread to Germany and the Low Countries. German paneling of this type could be quite elaborate, while the English developed a simpler style. A number of rooms in Elizabethan England were faced with untreated oak paneling that was inlaid with patterns of contrasting woods. An especially fine example of this style is the High Great Chamber in the Old House at Chatsworth, England, described in a household inventory of 1601 as "set forth with planets in coloured woods markentrie." It is also noted that another room was "very fayre waynscotted with coloured woods set out with portals." An even more notable surviving English example of this *intarsia* is the Inlaid Chamber at Sizergh Castle of the mid-sixteenth century. Inlaid with poplar and oak, the room's elaborate paneling is of a type that fell out of fashion in England in the seventeenth century and was replaced by simpler inlay, and particularly, star-shaped patterns.

Woods

Since the Middle Ages, the most frequently used woods for paneling have been oak and pine. A hard wood with a close grain, oak is generally pale in color, though dark varieties exist. Pine, a straight-grained yellow- or white-colored wood, varies from fairly hard to very soft. Relatively inexpensive, it can be carved and painted with ease. Having been popular from the Middle Ages until the late sixteenth century, oak was replaced by walnut as the wood of choice in France, and then in England almost a century later. A hard wood, walnut varies from light to dark brown and sometimes has black or dark brown veining. During the eighteenth century, beech, a straight-grained timber that is light brown to reddish brown in color, was widely used throughout Europe, especially in England. In Northern Europe, the principal woods used were oak and beech. Chiseled with precision to form high-relief panels, these readily available timbers were then varnished. When varnished, oak retains its light honey color and does not turn gray. Cypress and fruitwoods found favor throughout the Mediterranean. In the southern part of the region, soft woods, such as pine and larch, remain popular for their ease of handling and rustic charm.

Cedar, mahogany, maple, walnut, and cherry are among the other timbers chosen for works characterized by delicacy and complexity. There are also precious and exotic woods, such as rosewood, lemonwood, and cypress, which are reserved for especially exquisite paneling. Skillful artisans have also mimicked exotic timbers by painting wood graining. The hall at Chippenham, England, is a seventeenth-century example of paneling with exotic woods. In her notorious travel journals, Celia Fiennes described it as "wanscoated with walnut tree, the pannells and rims round with mulberry tree that is lemon coullour, and

OPPOSITE
This elaborate composite of wood moldings shows stenciling, carving, gilding, and inlay.

BELOW
Paneled in rough timber, this living room in a 1743 colonial house in Kent, Connecticut, belonging to architectural historian Jeffrey Morgan, is an example of early American design.

the moldings beyond it round are of a sweet outlandish wood not much differing from cedar but of a finer grain." The Great Chamber in the Mauritshuis, built in 1633 at The Hague, was also paneled in a rare wood, an Indian one that came from Brazil. Fiennes also reported that some of the paneling at England's Wimbledon House of 1649 was varnished green and decorated with golden stars and crosses. Such enhancements to wood paneling became an attractive option.

Painted Wood Graining and Faux Marble

Starting in the seventeenth century and continuing today, wood paneling was dressed up through wood graining—the painted imitation of timber, often a rare one or several mixed together to create a pattern. England's Ham House has examples of imitation olive wood and cedar. Celia Fiennes documented a parlor at Broadlands that was "wanscotted and painted a cedar coullour," while R. T. Gunther in his book *The Architecture of Sir Roger Pratt* (Oxford, 1928), mentioned the imitation of "prince's wood," a type of rosewood.

Wood graining was usually executed on "deal" paneling, relatively inexpensive and similar to modern plywood. Closely related to graining and equally popular during this period, marbling was known as "*marbre contrefait*" or "*marbre feint.*" Remarkable, early examples can still be viewed at England's Dyrham, Ham House, and Belton. Wood graining and faux marble were often mixed together in rooms of lesser importance, such as an antechamber, or used to decorate the lower part of staircase paneling or in a dining room. These painting methods owe some of their appeal to their relative affordability, compared to the exorbitant cost of rare woods.

The Paneled Library

Owing to its beauty and practicality, wood paneling was the wall treatment of choice for libraries in the seventeenth and eighteenth centuries. Libraries and studies continued the Renaissance *studiolo* tradition as important rooms storing prized collections. A sign of intellectual superiority, books were the main source of knowledge at the time. The common medieval practice of keeping one's books in a chest became impractical as libraries grew, giving rise to more bookcases. During the seventeenth century, books were hidden behind paneled doors, which were part of a greater wood paneling scheme. For example, in the Hôtel de Lauzun in Paris, built in about

The shell-shaped green niche in my Litchfield dining room is surrounded by a cabinet with a whimsical peach-toned faux-marble finish.

74

1660, books are housed in cupboards with doors that form an integral part of the richly painted paneling. As bookbinding had become a prestigious art, displaying the attractive spines on the shelves became important. Thus, bookcases fronted with wire mesh or panes of glass were designed. The bookcases in Milan's Ambrosian Library, built in 1603–09, have wire-mesh doors that are said to be original.

The well-known architect Jacques François Blondel (1667–1754) suggested that libraries are *"des pièces intimes, pour jouir de l'agreement de la lecture, lambris- sées avec des armoires de boiserie aux portes grillagées protegeant les ouvrages contre le vol"* (intimate rooms created to be able to enjoy reading, paneled with bookcases having wire-mesh doors in order to protect the books from being stolen). He adds that the inside of the shelves should have a dust pelmet. However, most libraries

OPPOSITE

At Caramoor this seventeenth-century paneled library from a château in Aveyron, France, has a vaulted ceiling illustrating stories from the Old Testament.

ABOVE

This detail shows painted door panels that depict a walled landscape and a neoclassical fountain with equine sculptures.

OPPOSITE

The painted, silvered, and gilded decorations of the Roman neoclassical library at Caramoor were conceived in 1802 by Filippo Santi of Perugia. The painted surfaces of the wood panels depict principal Roman sites.

ABOVE

This panel detail shows St. Peter's Square (Piazza San Pietro).

arranged their books on shelves that were installed on wood-paneled walls. In the many drawings by Daniel Marot (1661–1752), the French architect and engraver who worked for William of Orange, libraries with open bookcases used curtains in front of the shelves as a stylish protection for valuable books. Books in the *Boekcabinet* of 1700 at the Binnenhof in The Hague, were protected with white damask curtains and pelmets, while Ham House's library, which was fitted in the 1670s, is another fine example.

Refined and sophisticated libraries abound throughout Europe, many of them with painted decorations. In the small English library at Langley Marish, Bucks, for example, the overmantel is painted with grotesques, and the book cupboards have interiors painted with open books in *trompe l'oeil*. At the early twentieth-century New York villa Caramoor, there is a charming French library of 1678, which was built originally for a château in Aveyron, France. Its preserved wood-paneled walls and ceiling are covered with paintings of Old Testament stories about Saul, David, Gideon, and Samson, framed by baroque-style stone reliefs.

Throughout the centuries the library has reflected different decorative styles. Installed in Caramoor is a second library, an extraordinary neoclassical gem, imported in its entirety from Rome. Executed in 1802 by Filippo Santi of Perugia, its white-toned wood panels are enhanced with silver and gilded decorations. Painted on the paneled doors of the corner cabinets are the major sights of Rome—the ruins on the Via Appia, Piazza Navona, Trajan's Column, the Pantheon, Campidoglio, Castel Sant'Angelo, and Piazza San Pietro.

Libraries remain important rooms in a home with often a great amount of thought dedicated to make them beautiful and comfortable. Because wood shelves are still the best way to store and display books, wood paneling is still as relevant as ever.

Fireplace Mantels, Molding, and Mirrors

Fireplaces with mantels were part of a wood-paneled room's design. An essential source of heat and light, the fireplace remains a major feature of many rooms despite the introduction of central heating. Because it is a centerpiece, architects throughout the centuries have devoted much effort to the design of the fireplace to make it as striking and distinctive as possible. By the mid-1650s specific designs had become available in Paris. Jean Barbet's book *Livre d'Architecture* features many fireplace designs, and due to its popularity, was reissued several times in the mid-1600s.

The massive sixteenth-century *cheminée*, with its large, drafty opening, gradually evolved into a smaller and more elegant fireplace with a lower opening, limiting the potential for draft. The architectural elements surrounding the fireplace became less overpowering as evidenced by Jean Le Pautre's engravings *Cheminées à la moderne*, published in 1661. This tendency spread to Holland and England, and Daniel Marot published *Nouvelle cheminées à panneau de glace à la maniére de France* in about 1695. Some of the chimneypieces depicted can still be seen at Hampton Court and Kensington Palace. The fireplace surround eventually became a wood panel in keeping with the walls and moldings.

Molding is another important element of wood paneling. The finishing touch in a paneled room is crown molding (or a cornice), originally designed to hide the joint between the ceiling and the wall. Each period has produced a variety of crown-molding styles. Without the horizontal finality of a crown molding or the lyrical interest that a broken pediment or a dentil frieze provides, wood paneling can look unfinished—like a great painting without a frame. Crown molding provides a feeling of weight, linking architectural elements such as windows, doors, arches, and niches. Combinations of cove, quarter-round, and ogee moldings reflect light and create shadows that add visual interest.

A chair rail (also known as a dado) is a molding fixed horizontally to the wall around the perimeter of the room. Furnishings, especially chairs, were placed against walls in seventeenth- and eighteenth-century homes, and this rail offered protection. The architect Jean François Blondel insisted: "*On doit prendre garde que les contours inferieurs des panneaux ne tombent point assez bas pour que les dossiers des fauteuils puissent en derober la vue.*" (You have to be careful that the bottom of the molding is not too low so that it is not hidden by the back of the armchairs.) Traditionally thirty-six inches high, the chair rail could be higher with

OPPOSITE, ABOVE, LEFT
The fireplace in the bedroom of Dana and Fritz Rohn's eighteenth-century Litchfield County, Connecticut, farmhouse is painted an unexpected bright green.

OPPOSITE, ABOVE, RIGHT
A purple, painted wood-paneled fireplace with its matching walls create drama in Steven Gambrel's eighteenth-century house in Sag Harbor, New York.

OPPOSITE, BELOW
At Henry Sleeper's Beauport in Gloucester, Massachusetts, the Octagon Room has a chocolate-brown paneled fireplace surround with matching walls. The painted paneling is a vivid contrast to the red tôle collection, which is artfully placed on the mantle.

ABOVE

The textured paint in a pale shade of lavender on the wall of my sun porch in Litchfield, Connecticut, has been sponged and marbelized. Next to the semigloss white-painted chair rail, the color pops even more.

OPPOSITE

This pale gray New York City bedroom with white molding in a Stanford White-designed apartment exudes elegant simplicity. The upholstered chair and matching ottoman echo the color scheme of the walls.

taller ceilings. Today its purpose is mainly aesthetic for walls without the full wood-panel treatment. The chair rail is a practical finish, particularly in a space where paneling or plain walls suffer a lot of wear and tear. Wainscoting is simple paneling used to cover the part of walls below the chair rail.

During the late fifteenth century, the Venetians invented a brilliant, flat-glass mirror backed with an amalgam of mercury and tin. Mirrors became a great luxury of the time. They were often set into wood paneling. At her palace in Paris, Catherine de Medici (1519–80) had a *Cabinet de Miroirs* faced with no less than 109 plain Venetian mirrors inset in paneling. The mirrors, however, were quite small—the wood panels into which they were set were the predominant feature. Catherine de Medici even had a portrait of her husband Henry II, painted on glass, set above the fireplace. By 1670 many of the grand rooms of France and England had large areas of the walls entirely paneled with mirrors. When, in 1668, Louis XIV had an *appartement* decorated for his new mistress, Louise de La Vallière, the *Grand Cabinet* was faced with mirror glass set in wood panels—the latest fashion. The *Galerie des Glaces* at Versailles is the preeminent example of this splendid wall and wood-panel decoration, with mirrors made in French factories. This vogue also spread to England, where Jean-Baptiste Monnoyer (1634–99) worked for Queen Mary and painted a glass at Kensington Palace in London that was, according to Thomas Faulkner's *History and Antiquities of Kensington* of 1820, "tastefully decorated with festoons and flowers." This fashionable wall decoration, used in the most sophisticated rooms of Europe, continued throughout the centuries. Set into chimney breasts, mirrors also imparted a sense of lightness. The use of mirrors to brighten interiors is a decorating technique of enduring appeal.

The wood shell cabinet of the Golden Step Dining Room at Beauport, Henry Sleeper's home near the ocean, expands the room's nautical theme with maritime carvings and woodwork and furniture painted in sea-foam green.

OPPOSITE
The mirrored room with bamboo molding by Howard Brodsky harks back to Versailles's masterpiece, the Galerie des Glaces.

Boiseries

Boiserie is the French term for woodwork, including wood paneling. It usually describes seventeenth- and eighteenth-century carved and decorated wood paneling with shallow relief, carved foliage, and other ornate flourishes. In its most elaborate form, it is considered one of the highest expressions of woodcraft. During the sixteenth and seventeenth centuries, the traditional way of decorating important rooms included *boiseries* with tapestries hung from above. A rare, extant example can be found in the Louvre (the former Château du Louvre) in a room called *La Chambre de la Parade*. The finely proportioned, square wood panels from the older part of the castle have been carved with gilded trophies inspired by forms from antiquity. Faded tapestries belonging to Cardinal Mazarin hang above them.

By the seventeenth century wood paneling had gained prominence. Reception rooms in Europe, and later in America, were lined with paneling that was embellished with painted decorations and carving. The rules for such decorations were as follows: the baseboard was often painted in *faux marbre* in order to create a

separation between the parquet floor (usually waxed oak) and the *boiserie*. Painting was considered a sufficient protection against the wear and tear of daily use. The panels below chair-rail height were decorated in either *grisaille bas-relief* or with a *trompe l'oeil* design of flowers or fruits. The vertical panels above were painted with a landscape, vases full of flowers, or grotesques. Moldings and ceilings were also painted. This decorative scheme was a well-established one. Spectacular examples from the seventeenth century can be seen in the beautiful Hôtel Lambert in Paris, designed by Louis Le Vau. Mythological subjects are painted on the wood-paneled walls in the *Cabinets de l'Amour, des Muses,* and *des Bains.* In the magnificent *Chambre de la Presidente,* painted by Eustache Le Sueur and Charles Le Brun, are grotesques inspired by Raphael and reminiscent of ancient frescoes. The most pious and provincial people chose not to enhance their paneling with mythological scenes, which were too pagan for their taste; instead they commissioned images from the Old Testament. (Depictions of scenes from the New Testament were reserved for churches and monasteries.)

Painter-decorator Le Brun created an interior style that unified all of the decorative elements of a room. First at the baroque-style Château de Vaux-le-Vicomte, on the outskirts of Paris, Le Brun masterfully combined detailed mythological-inspired paintings, mainly on the ceilings, with elaborately carved, gilded, and painted wood paneling. This decorative panel scheme served as the model for the *Galerie d'Apollon* at the Château du Louvre, and then again at Versailles. Versailles enabled Le Brun to exercise the full scope of his genius with the Staircase of the Ambassadors (1674–78); the *Galerie des Glaces* (Hall of Mirrors; 1679–84); and the *Salons de la Guerre et de la Paix* (Salons of War and Peace; 1685–86). Each of his paintings, framed by elaborate wood paneling, glorifies the victories of King Louis XIV. Le Brun also oversaw the decoration of the *grand appartements,* which are enhanced with wood paneling of the finest materials. The fifty-something king also ordered paneling for his *appartement particulier,* which was *boise dans son entier* (paneled all over), as well as for the interior of the Trianon and his beloved Château de Marly, its exterior clad in rare marble with sophisticated *boiseries* inside.

Architects considered *boiseries* the best way to finish a room. The architect Augustin Charles Daviler (1653–1701) wrote in his well-known book *Cours d'Architecture* (1691):

> *Les boiseries rendent les lieux secs et chauds et, par conséquent, sains*
> *et habitables, peu de temps après qu'ils ont été bâtis; outre qu'ils*
> *épargnent les meubles dans les pièces d'une moyenne grandeur et les*

A view of a spectacular enfilade from a sumptuous wood-paneled living room in a private house in Paris, designed by Alberto Pinto.

plus fréquentées, car si elles sont boisées, il ne faut pour les meubler que quelques miroirs et tableaux qu'on attache sur les panneaux. Les boiseries servent encore à corriger les défauts dans les pièces comme un biais ou une enclave causé par quelque tuyau de cheminée à côté duquel on pratique des armoires dont les guichets (portes) conservent la même symétrie que le reste.

(Wood panels make every room dry and warm and therefore healthy and hospitable as soon as they have been built. In addition, in smaller rooms, less furniture is needed. In the larger rooms, only some mirrors and paintings need to be added. Wood panels also are very helpful in hiding imperfections in a room due to chimney pipes; you can cover them with doors to create symmetry.)

Trompe l'oeil designs in the boiserie style dress up this contemporary hallway painted in grisaille. The wood-paneled door complements the exquisite artistry.

And the English seventeenth-century writer Randle Holme stated that the walls of dining rooms ought to be "well wainscoted about, either with mountain and panells, or carved as the fashion was." The Swedish architect Daniel Cronström (1655–1719) observed that with paneling *"l'odeur des viandes ne se sentiroit point"* (the odor of food will not be smelled at all). This may be why small dining areas (no room was then exclusively used for dining) at the end of the seventeenth century were often paneled or sometimes hung with gilt leather.

Intricate *boiseries*, often painted and gilded, came to define sophisticated French interiors of the seventeenth and eighteenth centuries. The more extensively carved portions of the paneling were typically in the molding, while the central areas remained flat but were decorated with painted landscapes or portraits in tempera. Because paint is a practical way of hiding imperfections in the wood, it partly explains why painted panels became so fashionable. Often the paintings were done on canvas and then set in *boiserie* frames. *Boiseries* also extended beyond the walls to include doors, frames, and cupboards.

Blanc de Roi: White-Painted Boiseries

The Swedish envoy and architect Nicodemus Tessin, in a 1693 letter, wrote of the latest wood-panel craze in Paris: *"On ne peint les chambres boisées, les portes, les volets, les chassis, les plafonds, les portes, que de blanc avec le filet d'or ou sans o."* (One no longer paints paneled rooms, shutters, window frames, ceilings, and doors anything but white with or without narrow gilded moldings.) In most of the grand rooms at Versailles, the *boiseries* were painted white, with and without gold

enhancement. The white *boiseries* became known as *"blanc de roi."* Gilding dates back to antiquity. Since the Middle Ages in Europe, two methods have been used to overlay wood with gold leaf: oil gilding and water gilding. The less expensive and simpler oil gilding is more durable. Since it cannot be burnished, oil gilding lacks the luster of water gilding. The Versailles gilded decorations (*dorure à l'eau*) were water based, considered the best way to finish such sumptuous *boiseries.*

The fad of white-paneled rooms enhanced with gold continued well into the next century and was sometimes paired with pale *rechampie* (color combinations). Moldings were painted two or three different tones of yellow and blue or blue and pink. A stellar example is in the Hôtel de Toulouse in Paris, celebrated in eighteenth-century guidebooks for its architecture and decoration by François Mansart and Robert de Cotte. Between 1713 and 1719 most of the interiors were redesigned for the Comte de Toulouse. Later the Duc de Penthièvre made changes to the ground-floor arrangements for his daughter-in-law, the Princess de Lamballe. This *hôtel particulier* near the Place des Victoires was untouched until the Revolution with the princess's *appartement* an enchantment of late eighteenth-century decoration. Luc-Vincent Thiery de Sainte Colombe in his *Guide des Amateurs* of 1787 described the *salon* as ". . . the woodwork is painted white and gold in the modern manner."

Many complained bitterly that the *blanc de roi* and wood gilding was an over-the-top decoration for the living rooms of the nouveau riche, ruining the aristocracy. Others campaigned for a return to natural colors; the architect Daviler wanted to *"garder au bois sa couleur naturelle"* (keep the wood its natural color). Jacques François Blondel wrote in his *Cours d'architecture*: *"Pour l'amour du vrai, que les boiseries de chene fussent seulement cirées."* (For the love of truth the oak *boiseries* should be just waxed.) Consequently, in many private houses the main reception room was the only space painted white and enhanced with gilding, depending on the owner's budget. Less grand rooms were often painted with varnish to hide knots or irregularities. This led to the term *à la capucine* (a type of *faux-bois*) to describe wood paneling as grim as a Capuchin monk's cell and as drab as his brown robe.

The fashion for white-painted and gilded wood paneling in major reception rooms endured throughout the eighteenth century. Many palaces throughout Europe had wood panels painted white in their main reception rooms to better set off the fine carvings. An exquisite example of Bavarian rococo wood paneling is the circular, domed *Spiegelsaal* (Hall of Mirrors) in the Amalienburg-Nymphenburg Palace in Munich. The carved, painted, and gilded wood paneling designed by François Cuvilliés the Elder, has vivacious curves enhanced by mirrors and stucco.

The magnificent Hall of Mirrors, designed by François Cuvilliés (1695–1768) with stucco work by Johann Baptist Zimmermann (1680–1758), in the Schloss Nymphenburg, Munich, is an extravaganza of boiserie.

93

The Lacquer Room

Europe's fascination with China began in the thirteenth century, when Marco Polo returned from the East with fascinating tales of his adventures. When the first ambassador from Siam visited Versailles in 1682 and brought precious gifts, including red lacquered furniture, interest increased dramatically, sparking the eighteenth- and nineteenth-century fashion for what was known as *"chinoiserie."* This vogue expressed itself in all forms of wall decoration. Initially, entire lacquer panels were imported from China for fitting in furniture and on walls, but the supply was not sufficient. In response, new techniques of production were developed in Europe, tailored to satisfy the demand of the European market.

The French developed their own variation of lacquer, *vernis martin*, named after its creator Guillaume Martin and his three brothers. Many of Versailles's *petits appartements* were paneled with it. Dazzled by the brilliance of the Sun King's court, many German princesses decorated their *Schlösser* with a large staircase, a *galerie des glaces*, and a suite of *appartements*, some paneled with lacquer.

Throughout Europe *chinoiserie* was popular during the eighteenth century. In Portugal, Germany, and France, lacquer was considered an expression of princely magnificence along with gilding and rare marbles. Many English houses boasted lacquered rooms, including Burghley, Chatsworth, and Hampton Court. In

OPPOSITE

OPPOSITE

The dark, lacquer-
paneled walls of Vienna's
Schloss Schönbrunn's
round Chinese Cabinet
boldly contrast with the
bright, white-painted wood
paneling accented in gold.
Small consoles support
blue-and-white porcelain
vases in an impressive
example of European
chinoiserie from the
eighteenth century.

RIGHT

The double entrance
doors to Caramoor's
blue dining room are
lacquered with fanciful
"Chinese" designs,
combined with a lustrous
inset mirror above, and
originally created for
the Venetian palace
Ca' Rezzonico in the
mid-eighteenth century.
This special lacquering
technique is known
as lacca contraffatta
(or arte povera).

Italy palaces and villas had Chinese rooms in lacquer (known as *lacca contraffatta* or *arte povera*). This process included several steps: decoupage decorations were applied to a wall, enhanced with painted designs, then covered with many coats of lacquer. The particular charm of Venetian lacquer resides in its coarse quality, creating a more exuberant decoration, such as the pair of double doors lacquered with festive Chinese scenes in gilt made for the Venetian palace Ca' Rezzonico in the 1750s. Painted with such assured elegance, the doors are considered the work of the master painter Tiepolo or his son.

High-quality lacquer continued to be a favorite wood finish throughout the next centuries. Its sumptuousness defines luxury. At the start of the twentieth century, Jean Dunand (1877–1942), a Swiss designer and expert in lacquerwork, created art deco–inspired wonders much sought after by wealthy collectors.

THE SPLENDOR OF FRANCE

Gilt Leather

First produced in the Islamic world in the seventeenth century, gilt leather appeared as a striking form of wall decoration. Moorish Spain developed this technique, often referred to as *cordou* (or Cordova) leather. The center of production eventually moved to the Low Countries, with Malines and Amsterdam particularly famous for their leathers. Also produced in France, and to a lesser extent in England, Italy, and Portugal, gilt leather was not, in fact, gilt at all but made of calfskin faced with tinfoil. During the late seventeenth century, these skins were embossed by pressing a wooden mold carved in intaglio with a pattern (a version of a stencil technique). The ground was often punched with small patterns that reflect the light. With the main design painted in one or more colors, these skins were made into wall hangings of any specified size. Border patterns were also created, and narrow strips of the material hid the nails that held the hangings in place. Essentially an early form of wallpaper, gilt leather sometimes paired with wood paneling, became popular in Dutch houses during the seventeenth and eighteenth centuries.

OPPOSITE
Painted walls that simulate stamped leather surround this sumptuously decorated Parisian living room designed by Alberto Pinto.

BELOW
The painted walls of this New York City sitting room imitate stamped leather.

Fretwork, Cutwork, and Latticework

Fretwork, also known as cutwork or latticework, is another way to enhance paneled rooms. This intricate or simple framework of crisscrossed strips of wood is applied to paneling or used without it. Purely ornamental or used as a support, it simulates the trellises in an outdoor garden room. An ancient technique practiced by the Egyptians, it was embraced by the Chinese and again in Europe during the *chinoiserie* rage and the Gothic era. Fretwork has been chosen for some of the most superb, playful rooms throughout Europe during the eighteenth and nineteenth centuries. The garden pavilion at Neues Schloss in Bayreuth, Germany, with its magnificent trelliswork arbor of climbing roses is an important example as is the Faisandrie, also decorated with charming roses, in Chantilly, France. Another wonderful eighteenth-century example is the game room in Palermo's Palazzina La Favorita, which has a ceiling of painted trelliswork. In America, the twentieth-century decorator Tony Duquette famously used fretwork to create memorable garden rooms.

BELOW

The intricate latticework design of this towering garden pavilion spans multiple doors, which open on stunning views of the hilly landscape. Reminiscent of a Chinese pagoda, it was designed by Michael Booth for Nan McEvoy's ranch in Marin County, California.

OPPOSITE

The elaborate trelliswork on the walls of Dodie Rosekrans's San Francisco dining gazebo is amplified in size on the ceiling.

The Folk Tradition

Due to their practicality, painted wood panels proliferated in simple country dwellings throughout northern European countries, ranging from Germany and Austria to Sweden and Denmark. Timber was plentiful and practical, so the inside walls were paneled for additional comfort. As most farmhouses in Northern Europe were built of wood, many reflected the long tradition of decoratively painted wood walls.

The walls of the common *stube* (parlor or main living space) were typically paneled from floor to ceiling in northern Germany, Swabia, Tyrol, and Switzerland, while in Franconia, half-height wainscoting was generally the norm. In most areas of Germany, the better houses would have a second *gute stube* (good parlor) used only for special occasions. They had their own regional names: in Franconia, they were called "little cabinets," a direct reference to the *studiolo* of the Renaissance.

Different countries share design traditions, as they do religious imagery originating from the Bible and depicted on the walls of churches and monasteries. Church paintings often date from the late Middle Ages or the Renaissance and are often frescoes. Another source of inspiration—local flora and fauna—is secular. The decorations are freehand designs with cutouts or stencils employed for efficient execution. Wallpaper or canvas was expensive and hard to come by, whereas color pigments, chalk, and glue were cheap and plentiful.

Most farmers had cows and milk, which was used to create casein paint—from skimmed sour milk—a very stable base. The paint was then mixed with lime and colored with the juices of cornflowers for blues or purple and strawberries or raspberries for shades of red and pink. The wood panel was prepared with a thin coat of plaster prior to the application of paint. Used in most rural areas well into the nineteenth century, casein was gradually replaced by oil paint.

The best parlors were decorated with either panels or paintings, such as the oak panels of Friesian houses carved with birds and flowers, many painted blue to match the popular color of Dutch ceramic tile. Near Hamburg, where many fruit trees grow, the preference was for ornately inlaid panels that originated in Swabia and Tyrol. In areas where farmers were less wealthy, the panels had cutouts and painted motifs, usually done by itinerant artists.

Murals of astounding quality have survived from the early sixteenth and seventeenth centuries. In northern Germany, scenes were copied from the engravings in illustrated bibles. In private homes, self-educated farmers often chose

These details of a rustic 1796 painted Bavarian armoire and canopy bed from Caramoor's collection hail from a long tradition of depictions of saints and bouquets of flowers. Similar religious and secular designs appear on walls in this part of the world.

imagery from the lives of the saints and combined it with stylized leaves, floral motifs, branches, and simple architectural designs of circles or squares. Another popular motif was the Tree of Life, inspired by the Renaissance. In Sweden during the late seventeenth century, this image was reprised as an interest in botany

swept the country due to the popularization of exotic flower engravings. An equally widespread image was the allegory of the four seasons, giving agriculture its annual structure, along with a myriad of floral motifs. To balance heavily decorated walls, the furniture was simpler and painted in complementary colors.

Wood paneling continued to have aficionados around the world. In America the legendary Elsie de Wolfe (1865–1950), in *The House in Good Taste* (1913), gave an endorsement to it, throwing in some very wise advice: "Lately there has been a great revival of interest in wood paneling. We go abroad, and see the magnificent paneling of old English homes, and we come home and copy it. But we cannot get the workmen who will carve panels in the old patterns. We cannot wait a hundred years for the soft bloom that comes from the constant usage, and so our paneled rooms are apt to be too new and woody. But we have such a wonderful store of woods, here in America, it is worthwhile to panel our rooms, copying the single rectangular English patterns, and it is quite permissible to age our walls by rubbing in black wax, and little shadows of watercolor, and in fact by any method we can devise. Wood-paneled walls, like beamed ceilings, are best in great rooms. They make boxes of little ones."

Wainscoting, Tongue-and-Groove Planks, and Beadboard

A simple design of local wood applied to the wall achieves a clean, warm look. One such basic form is wainscoting, a plain paneling placed between a baseboard and a chair rail on an interior wall. Wainscoting comes in a variety of types—a raised or flat panel, simple plank, or beadboard. Traditional wainscoting consists of tongue-and-groove boards nailed vertically up the wall.

The term "wainscoting" is derived from the fourteenth-century Dutch/Flemish word *waghenscote*. Traced back to sixteenth-century England, it was applied to the lower interior sections of stone walls of houses to prevent cold drafts. Throughout the eighteenth and nineteenth centuries, wainscoting primarily adorned simple dwellings. In fact, the walls of many early American farmhouses have humble, unpainted flat paneling.

Easy to install and relatively inexpensive, the natural grain of plain pine planks or other common wood is appealing for a country house. Wide tongue-and-

109

BELOW, LEFT

*Designers Diamond and
Baratta jauntily placed
weather vanes on the
planked wall of this
Southampton bathroom.*

BELOW, RIGHT

*The home of Ilya Repin,
near St. Petersburg, Russia,
has a striking horseshoe-
shaped window, with
fanned boards around a
trellised glass window.*

OPPOSITE

*The surfaces of interior
designer Eric Prokesh's
studio alcove in Dallas,
Texas, have a verdigris finish.*

groove planks, placed vertically or horizontally, and beadboard are alternatives. Often painted white or a light color, beadboard creates a fresh, clean look. Today, wainscoting is an attractive way to enhance the decor of a room and can even disguise areas with imperfections.

Throughout its long history, the variety of wood paneling has been immense; the common denominator is the use of carved and painted wood. Whether made of pine, fruitwood, or some other species, wood paneling is a versatile way to adorn a room. Bear in mind, however, that the height and design need to be carefully calculated to fit a space. In fact, historically, a pattern was often drawn on the wall in black chalk to ensure that the paneling fits the room, a technique still in use today.

Centuries have rolled by, and wood paneling in a variety of finishes has endured the changing fashions. Many extant rooms in museums as well as in private houses throughout the world stand as testament to a luxurious world gone by and serve as an inspiration for a beautiful future.

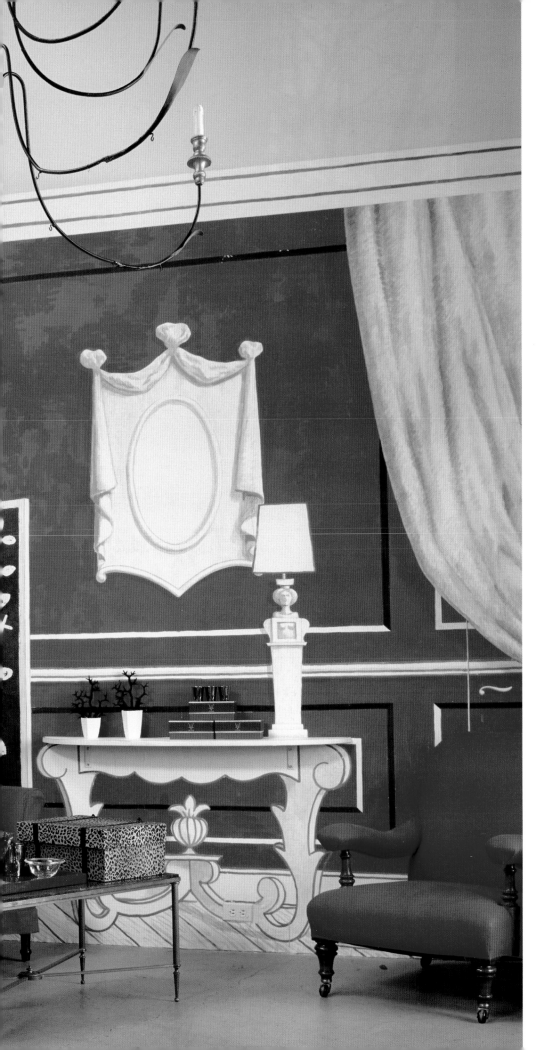

A whimsical example of faux wood paneling and molding, this painted backdrop by French painter Paulin Paris makes a unique holiday decoration for Hollyhock, Suzanne Rheinstein's decorative arts and antiques store in West Hollywood, California.

113

WOOD PANELING ESSENTIALS

With its beautiful textures, graining, and colors, wood has been used to decorate homes for centuries. Originally an elegant means of insulation, paneling eventually was custom-made for each room, involving the creation of intricate moldings, overmantels, door panels, and decorative framing for windows and doors.

The width and direction of simple wooden panels can change the proportions of a room, transforming a space. Be mindful of practical considerations such as the position of doors, window frames, and light switches. In successful paneled rooms, there is always a balance between the walls and the furniture.

PROTECTIVE FINISHES

Today's products can help to effectively protect wood paneling. Choose a finish appropriate to the room. Following are some attractive possibilities:

VARNISHING, STAINING, WAXING, AND FAUX FINISHES
Completely refinish the surface if the wood paneling is particularly dirty or scratched. Use a fine-grained sandpaper to remove recent layers of varnish or wax. To give paneling a fresh look, use a stain with a dark or light tonality, or apply a new layer of varnish or wax. Be creative and enhance the wood with a faux finish such as marbleizing.

GLUE PAINT
An old-fashioned method for coloring wood panel, glue paint uses hide glue to achieve a soft finish like velvet. The result, a warm and charming finish, is similar to lime. Totally absorbed in the raw wood, glue paint has the great advantage of never peeling.

MILK PAINT
This is another old-fashioned method for painting raw wood. For best results, wipe the wood surface with a damp rag to raise the grain before applying the first coat. Once dry, smooth down with very fine sandpaper.

CARE AND MAINTENANCE

Wood paneling requires periodic dusting. Regardless of the finish, gently vacuum paneling regularly with a brush attachment; alternatively, use a dusting wand or a microfiber dusting cloth. Always remove dirt completely; otherwise, it may become embedded in layers of wood polish, wax, or other restorative products. When ornately carved paneling has cracked or chipped, consult a professional restorer.

LEFT: This detail of a gray-blue gilded door is from a magnificent Parisian home designed by Alberto Pinto. ABOVE: This elegant eighteenth-century carved pediment molding is from Colonial Williamsburg's Governor's Palace. OPPOSITE: Designer Jacques Garcia's living room in the Château de Champs de Bataille showcases elaborate eighteenth-century wall decoration with portraiture in gold frames.

stencil

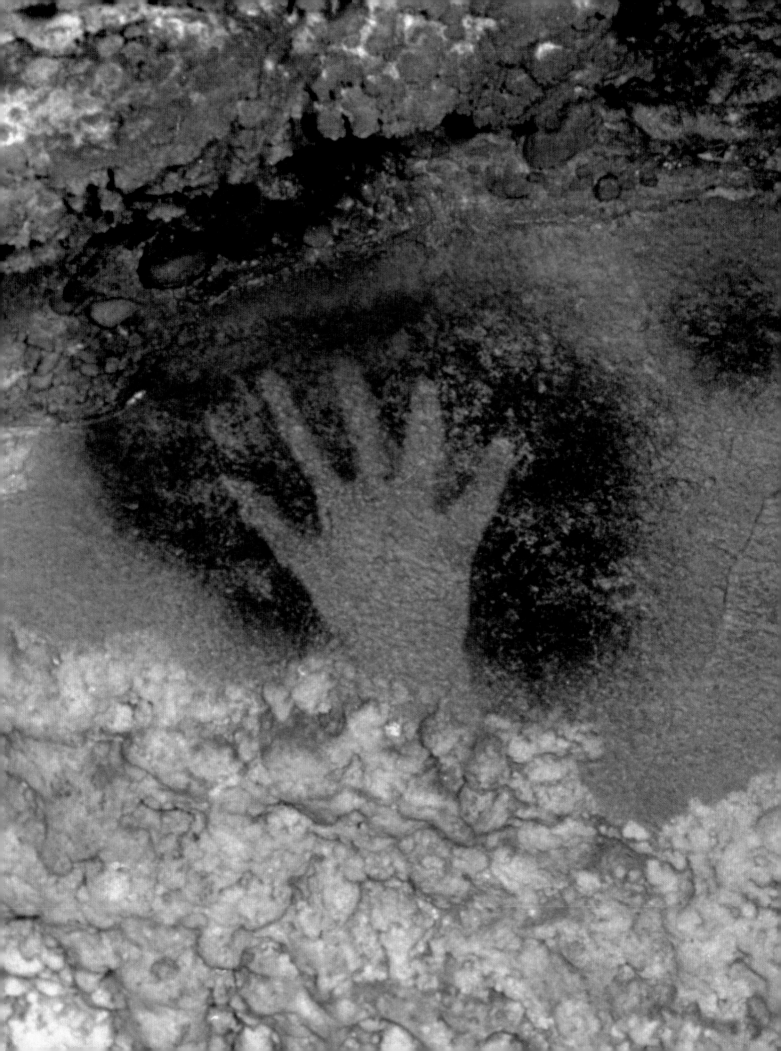

Stencil comes from the old French verb *estenceler* (to sparkle or cover with stars) and before that, from the Latin word *scintilla* which means spark. This makes sense—a stencil definitely adds an extra something, wherever it is placed. A beautiful, yet practical method of decorating a wall, stenciling is relatively inexpensive but requires a certain level of skill in the designing and cutting process. A pattern is created on a thin sheet of metal, leather, oilcloth, or most recently a semitransparent film like plastic or Mylar. The design is perforated into the selected material, then positioned on the wall surface and brushed over with paint or pigment. The color fills the parts of the surface that are exposed by the perforation, reproducing the pattern, for example of a leaf, on a wall.

Describing exactly what a stenciled wall refers to isn't clear-cut. Painted walls with repetitive designs can be misconstrued as stenciled designs. Not all repetitive patterns are stenciled; some are drawn freehand. To add to the confusion, stencils are often mixed with other decorative schemes. For example, they can be used for making a mural border or to create the printed repetitive patterns that appear on wallpaper.

Characterized by repetitive motifs, stenciling appears throughout antiquity. In fact, the urge to communicate through images coincides with man's earliest artistic expressions, which date back to the Paleolithic caves of 22,000 B.C. The famous Grotte de Lascaux is decorated with animal imagery enhanced with simple repetitive imprints of hands and feet. In the Fiji Islands, indigenous people created stencils by cleverly cutting holes into banana leaves that were then rubbed with vegetable dyes through the openings onto bark cloth (*tapa*).

In ancient Egypt artisans stenciled the outline of the figure or hieroglyph onto the walls of tombs; the stenciled outline was then incised in low relief. Next, a thin layer of stucco was placed on the surface to receive the paint. The Egyptians chose bright primary colors—mainly black, red, blue, and yellow. Inspired by nature, their designs often embodied an additional layer of meaning. For example, lotus and papyrus, which grew on the banks of the Nile, were popular images that symbolized food for the body and soul, while the feathers of rare birds represented the emblems of sovereignty. Unlike the Egyptians, the Greeks favored simple, stylized designs that were purely decorative. The walls of ancient Greek villas and clay vessels abound with stenciling, a testament to the high esteem in which it was held, not only by scribes and artisans but also by rulers and intellectuals. The remnants of clay vessels are in such renowned collections as the Metropolitan Museum of Art, The British Museum, and the Louvre, and on the walls of La Villa Kérylos in the South of France. Stenciling in ancient Rome had practical applications as well; Quintilian, the famous Roman preceptor of the first century A.D., used it to teach boys to write. Even the road signs of Rome had stenciled lettering.

The ancient cultures of Asia also embraced the art of stenciling. In China, stencils of Buddha are abundant, covering the walls of many shrines and caves as a means of spreading the Buddhist religion. Japanese artisans produced refined designs on fabric and later on hanging paper scrolls that decorated the walls of guest rooms. The Japanese borrowed this Chinese technique, imbuing it with a different sensibility using delicate stylized images from nature, such as cherry blossoms and gingko leaves.

Throughout the ages, stencils continued to serve both decorative and practical purposes. Some lesser-known uses included kings' signage on important documents. Theodoric the Great (454–526 A.D.), ruler of the Barbarian Ostrogoths, had been known to trace the first four letters of his name through a stencil cut in a thin plate of gold. And King Charlemagne (742–814 A.D.), emperor of the Franks, used stencils to sign official documents given to his *missi dominici* (envoys).

Papermaking, Woodcuts, Engravings, and Stencils

The Chinese invention of paper, believed to occur in the second century A.D., increased the usage of stencils for decorative purposes. The Muslims introduced paper manufacturing to Spain in the tenth century. From there, paper traveled to Sicily in the twelfth century, Italy in the thirteenth century, and France in the fourteenth century. Such exchanges between East and West, brought about

The library wall of La Villa Kérylos in Beaulieu-sur-mer, France (now a museum), is stenciled with laurels and a modified Greek key design. Around this room, medallions commemorate Greek poets, orators, and philosophers.

by the crusades and by expanding commerce, enriched the life of the common man. Stenciling served an important role in the creation of leisure activities such as card playing. Throughout Europe, as early as the fifteenth century, both the invention of playing cards and printed paper had a significant impact on the life of human beings. Their evolution ran parallel to each other, and both often were created in the same artisan workshop. It is believed that playing cards made from woodblocks originated in fifteenth-century Germany and migrated to Italy, France, and then Spain. The term *kartenmaler* (card painter) was first found on a document of 1402 from Ulm. Unfortunately, few examples of early playing cards decorated with hand-painted stenciling survive. The simple, one-color shapes, each designating a particular suit, lent themselves easily to stenciling for limited mass production.

German woodcuts and engravings were the forerunners to printed matter—printed material produced by printers or publishers. The earliest prints, dating from the fifteenth century, usually represent biblical scenes with dual instructional and decorative purposes. They were sanctioned by the Church and spread among the people to fortify their faith. Pope Boniface IX (1356–1404) had extended the grant of indulgences beyond Rome, including several cities in Germany and France. The number of pilgrims increased as there were more locations available to which to make pilgrimages. The Church made sure that religious prints found willing buyers at each shrine. These mass-produced devotional images (alluding to divine protection) were offered at the places of worship where thousands of people gathered. The Germans even developed a saying at the time: *"Alle zwolf apostle auf einen streich machen"* (to paint all the apostles at one stroke). Stencils enhanced this religious printed imagery, which graced the walls of its purchasers' simple dwellings. A French Virgin and Child with the young Saint Anne (c. 1500, The British Museum)—colored in red, green, and yellow—indicates how widely distributed this method was, appealing to noble and peasant alike.

By the early sixteenth century, painted stencils enlivened the coloring of block prints and became the established method. Examples have survived, including a German woodblock print known as *Der Briefmaler*, designed by Jost Amman (born in Zurich 1535). It depicts a painter at work in his shop stenciling image prints with brushes and colors at his side. This technique eventually led to the manufacture of wallpaper.

In France the wood engravers were known as *dominotiers*, and their colored papers as *dominos*. The *Encyclopedie* of 1765 defines *domino* sheets as "a paper on which the tracing, designs or figure are first printed with clumsy wooden blocks. The colors are applied afterwards by means of a *patron* or stencil." These decorative colored prints, intended for the homes of the bourgeois and peasants, cost a few pennies. Printed-paper imagery was pasted on cardboard for games such as lotto, dames, or tarots. The *dominotiers* also stenciled banners, ballad sheets, and pattern papers, which evolved into sophisticated stenciled wallpapers, especially in the capable hands of the Frenchman Jean-Michel Papillon (1661–1723). He refined the technique using watercolor washes and ink. Stencils were also used for large-scale flocking, a sophisticated wallpaper with repetitive designs created on cut ground velvet, requiring several woodblocks to print. The Englishman Robert Dossie in *The Handmaid to the Arts* (London, 1758) described fabrication for "the common kinds of wallpaper . . . it is usual to print only the outlines and to lay on the rest of the colours by stenciling, which both saves expense of cutting prints and can be done by common workmen."

Early European and British Stenciled Wall Designs and Motifs

Eventually stenciling became an integral part of wall decoration. In fourteenth-century churches and country castles of central France, the letters *HIS* (a Christogram) and diminutive motifs inspired by nature (such as leaves) appeared on walls, rafters, and ceilings. A magnificent stenciled quatrefoil from the fourteenth century is still visible in the refectory of the Abbaye de l'Epau. Stencils showed up more and more in French country castles during the following three centuries. Door frames and their panels were decorated with stenciled designs in monochromatic colors or in grisaille. Inset panels of wood or canvas were hand painted with religious scenes enhanced by stenciled borders as seen in the Chalmazel room of the Château de Saint-Marcel-de-Félines, near the Massif Central, a mountainous region in south-central France. The seventeenth-century wood paneling at Caramoor, an early twentieth-century Mediterranean-style villa in the outskirts of New York City, is painted with depictions of the Old Testament figures Saul, David, Gideon, and Samson, and framed with stenciled decoration.

In Italy and France, freehand decorations often accompanied stencils on churches or castle walls. Introduced during the Middle Ages in England, stenciling was not in vogue until the fifteenth century. At this time, stenciled patterns in relief on mural decoration—stars, *fleur-de-lys*, *soleil-en-splendour* (a radiating sun), and monograms became popular on the walls of many churches. Although few examples have survived, contemporary drawings and engravings of the time show these simple schemes were also common in domestic buildings.

Wood paneling together with plastered walls were the perfect surface on which to add color ornamentation. A portion of paneling from a church in Suffolk, from the fifteenth century (in London's Victoria and Albert Museum), shows eight panels with backgrounds painted alternatively in green and red and decorated with floral designs, including the thistle and the lily in white or yellow. The thistle represents nobility, while the lily symbolizes the Virgin Mary. At St. William's College in York, England, a painted chamber from the fifteenth century has plaster walls decorated completely with stenciling. Such repetitive patterns that cover an entire wall reoccur in Colonial America.

By the sixteenth century, the Painter-Stainers Company of London, a trade group, described stencils as "a deceitful work and destructive of creative painting, being a great hinderer of ingenuousness, a cherisher of idleness and laziness in all the said art." After stenciling received such harsh criticism, it nearly disappeared. In seventeenth-century England, however, it re-emerged with new designs that are less naturalistic and more geometric, such as squares and lozenges.

Eighteenth-century Neoclassical and the Adamesque Style

In the eighteenth century, Robert Adam (1728–92), a revered architect of Great Britain, was one of the first to take interior decoration seriously. He studied in Italy, from 1754 to 1758, where he developed a passion for classical antiquity. When he returned to England, Adam brought back knowledge of Roman monuments and enlisted a number of talented painters to work with him, among them Angelica Kaufmann, Antonio Zucchi, and Michelangelo Pergolesi. Together with his brother James, Adam built country estates for English patrons, with interior wall decorations of ancient Roman wreaths, *paterae* (circular architectural ornaments inspired by ancient Greek and Roman saucerlike vessels), honeysuckle vines, and fans. With painted walls in hues of pea green, sky blue, lemon, lilac, and bright pink, set off with elaborate plaster friezes, panels, and medallions, Adam harmonized walls with ceilings in his comprehensive decorative scheme. Several techniques were combined within one room to create a maximum effect. Sometimes landscape scenes and figurines were painted directly on paper or copper and applied to walls as

This detail from a stylized, organic stencil pattern on a plaster wall, dating from around the fifteenth century, is from the King's Room of the Treasurer's House in York, England.

seen in the Etruscan room at England's Osterley Park. Describing this particular room, Robert Adam claimed that "the style of the ornament and the coloring are both evidently imitated from the vases and urns of the Etruscan." Together with stenciled designs of vases, griffins, and muses as well as applied stucco decorations, these neoclassical wall schemes were all the rage. In a lecture delivered in 1812, the English architect Sir John Soane stated: "The light and elegant ornaments, the varied compartments in the ceilings of Mr Adam, imitated from Ancient Works in the Baths and Villas of the Romans, were soon applied in designs for every other species of furniture. . . . To Mr Adam's taste in the ornament of his buildings, and furniture we stand indebted . . ."

There were two British schools of neoclassicism. The first began with the whimsical fantasy of Robert Adam and his followers and the second with the classicism of the merchant banker and art collector Thomas Hope (1769–1831). In *Household Furniture and Interior Decoration* of 1807, Hope championed a more historically accurate classicism. To create a structured environment for his collection of ancient sculpture and vases, his stencils were pure reconstructions of actual Greek friezes and Egyptian hieroglyphics, influenced by the French Empire style of the architects Charles Percier and Pierre Fontaine. Classical mythology provided a wealth of inspiration, including parades of demigods and nymphs. Percier and Fontaine, who reigned over France's decorative arts for the first fifteen years of the nineteenth century, strove "to imitate the spirit, principles, and wisdom of antiquity" (from the preface of their book *Recueil des décorations intérieures*, 1812). Like Adam, they achieved a unified look by designing not only a building but also the interior decorative scheme: the selection of paint colors, curtain fabrics, and furniture. They enhanced rooms with friezes and panels with delicate repetitive motifs of sphinx, bees, and lyres. However, it is difficult to determine what parts of the friezes and panels were stenciled or handpainted.

The neoclassical vogue also spread to Russia and Scandinavia. A splendid example is the Pavlovsk Palace, a country residence of the Russian Imperial family outside of St. Petersburg. Completed in 1825 and heavily restored in the 1950s, this

OPPOSITE
Scottish designer Robert Adam created the Etruscan dressing room at England's Osterley Park in the mid-eighteenth century. Painted urns and sphinxes based on Pompeian designs, as well as stenciling, adorn the spirited green wall surface.

ABOVE
This Parisian study's wall decoration was inspired by Osterley Park's dressing room.

Crustaceans painted in marine blue enliven the fantastic wood panels by Andrei Voronikhin in St. Petersburg's Stroganov Palace.

OPPOSITE

Walls in faux marbre bordered with neoclassical motifs define the 1816 Carlo Rossi–designed corner salon of the Russian Imperial family's Pavlovsk Palace. The elegant marble goddess is at home in this environment.

summer estate has glorious lavender-colored stucco walls with stenciled and hand-drawn griffins and lyres. The Stroganov Palace of St. Petersburg also has rooms decorated with neoclassical-style design motifs.

France, Italy, and Northern European Stenciling

Wood paneling and plastered surfaces were best for showing off the beauty of stencil design. However, during the eighteenth and nineteenth centuries throughout France, Italy, and Scandinavia, stenciling was also executed on wall-mounted canvas.

In Northern European countries at the end of the seventeenth century, stenciling became the prominent form of wall decoration, informed by the folk

Neoclassical in its symmetry, this Italian stenciled frieze at Caramoor features ribbons and stalks of wheat, which create a lively effect.

This neoclassical stencil frieze of griffins and urns, dating from the early 1800s, decorates the main dining room in the refectory of a country house in Medivi, Sweden.

traditions of the area. The great centers of stenciling were in the Bavarian Alps, Franconia, the alpine regions of Austria and Switzerland, Tyrol, Alsace, France's Vosges, Saxony, and Silesia. Often applied to wood paneling in the *stube* (parlor or main living space), stenciling was the dominant decorative feature, along with painted furniture. Early stenciling from around 1600, particularly in Bavaria, was simple and repetitive. Drawn with a compass on wood panels, ornamentation consisted of stars and roses with arabesques and floral designs stenciled above. Mural paintings were gradually introduced, colors brightened, and the range of stenciled elements expanded to figures as well as stylized plant and floral motifs.

Beginning in the early seventeenth century, itinerant painters from the Dalecarlian region of central Sweden favored acanthus leaf motifs. They chose their

The imagery on the interior walls of Bavarian homes extends to the rustic painted and stenciled designs on the wooden furniture, such as these floral compositions from Caramoor's collection.

From the pineapple and leaf border to the willow tree separated by vines, naïve stenciling adds charm to the walls of the Kreuter House in Washington, Connecticut.

stencil motifs from two sources—religious and botanical. As the eighteenth century drew to a close, fashionable interiors of the period's manor houses became more well known. Thus, Swedish decorative painters began imitating these sophisticated schemes and frequently stenciled them in colors that complimented the furnishings.

Colonial America's Stenciling Tradition

Perhaps more than any other time and place, the stencil craft was popularized in Colonial America. Stenciling appeared shortly after the conclusion of the Revolutionary War, partly in response to the evolution of interior walls from rough-hewn timber to plaster. For a number of reasons, stenciling became the alternative to wallpaper. First, it was considered cleaner than wallpaper, which could conceal insects or other household vermin. Rufus Porter, the well-known itinerant painter and stenciler who traveled up and down the East Coast from 1825 to 1845, said that wallpaper "is apt to get torn off, and often affords behind it a resting place for various kind of insects." The second advantage was that stenciling could be applied directly to freshly cured plaster walls like fresco in contrast to wallpaper, which cannot be adhered until the wall is completely dry, a process that takes from six months to a year. Otherwise, the wallpaper will peel off the surface. Perhaps most significantly, stenciling was accomplished more easily and quickly and was less expensive than wallpapering.

During this time, many artists emigrated from England or the German Palatinate to America, and some became skilled in stenciling. The popular printed wallpapers of England inspired their stenciled wall patterns. Traveling with brushes, dry pigments, and rolls of stenciled patterns cut into heavy brown paper or leather stiffened with oil, these itinerant painters bartered their work for food, lodging, and even the skimmed milk used to make their paint.

Derived from nature, popular designs included leaves, fruits, wildflowers, vines, trees, birds, and stars, but the range of stencil motifs was endlessly imaginative. Many were symbols: flower baskets represented friendship; the oak leaf, strength and loyalty; the willow, everlasting life; and the pineapple, hospitality. The swag and pendant, known as the Liberty Bell, was a strong patriotic emblem. Simple parlor rooms were gussied up with charming borders of flowering roses outlining the windows and doors, while laurel leaves, swags, and tassels combined with geometric shapes created wide friezes to edge the ceilings. From about 1778 to the end of the first quarter of the nineteenth century, similar design motifs spread throughout the young nation—from Ohio to Connecticut and from New York to Maine.

OVERLEAF

Sheila Camera Kotur's country house in New England was originally built as an inn and tavern in 1780. Kotur restored the original stenciling in this master bedroom to its former beauty with watercolors. The detail of a red vase filled with flowers is an example of a classic, early American stencil decoration, which can be seen in many New England houses. This design is similar to that of the overmantel in the Josiah Sage House in South Sandisfield, Massachusetts.

133

The parlor of the 1797 Hichox House in Washington, Connecticut, is one of the finest extant examples of American wall stenciling, most likely by "Stimp." The tasseled festoons and the climbing vines bring a light, playful touch to the well-balanced design.

These stencilers achieved great success and beauty with crude, homemade materials that were difficult to use. They mixed paint from skimmed milk, lime, oil, and whiting (white chalk ground very fine) and added pigment to produce vibrant and eclectic colors. A thrifty artist produced as many colors as possible himself to avoid buying expensive pigment. For red, he boiled iron filings or brick dust or extracted the juice of pokeweed berries (aptly called the red ink plant), which grew by the side of the road. Black was obtained from soot (Rufus Porter mixed it with rum) or by burning nutshells in a pan, then grinding them with oil or varnish. Yellow was made from clay, which was also the base for the pale green, lavender, and plum that Rufus Porter favored. Blue came from the indigo plant, which was cultivated in the South and often sold by salesmen. A green pigment called verdigris was procured from the green rust of copper. Stencils colored in red and green were commonly applied to raspberry pink, salmon, gray, and ochre walls. The most prolific of the early stencilers and the best known was Moses Eaton, Jr. (1796–1886). Few stencilers signed walls, so most are unknown today. Eaton's decorative layout was carefree; he treated each wall as a separate space, eliminating the traditional frieze as a unifying element. Instead, he framed his stenciled vertical and horizontal spaces with doors and windows. He applied motifs more often by eye than by careful measurement. Through a fortunate happenstance, Eaton's kit with seventy-eight stencils was discovered in the 1930s, making his work identifiable.

Stenciling was a prominent feature in many Connecticut houses. One of the finest examples of wall stenciling adorns the parlor of the Hickox House in Washington. The curve of the climbing vines creates a sense of lightness in its well-balanced spacing. Built in 1797, this room of singular beauty and taste was most likely stenciled by a man called "Stimp" (perhaps short for Stimpson). Not much is known about him.

In contrast, Rufus Porter (1792–1884) had a well-documented life, with his boyhood spent in Bridgton, Maine. An artist and inventor, this self-taught, itinerant painter created stencil-enhanced frescoes of the young nation's villages and landscapes and is credited with helping shape America's culture. Eaton and Porter became friends and even worked on houses together. Porter passed on helpful hints regarding his own technique:

> The painting of houses, arbors, villages etc. . . . is greatly facilitated by
> means of stencils. . . . For this purpose several stencils must be made
> to match each other; for example one piece may have the form of a

front of a dwelling-house or other building cut through it; another piece may have the form of the end of the same house as viewed from an oblique direction; a third piece may be cut to represent the roof; and a fourth may be perforated for the windows. Then by placing them successfully on the wall and painting the ground through the apertures with a large brush, and with such colors as the different parts require, the appearance of a house is readily produced in a nearly finished state.

Porter could paint the four walls of a room, creating fancy scenes, trees, and villages, in about five hours. No wonder these fanciful stenciled images were so popular—the technique was quick and relatively inexpensive. In the Rufus Porter Museum in Bridgton, Maine, the Westwood murals from Dr. Francis Howe's home in Westwood,

OPPOSITE
The eagle, urns, and suns stand out in this 1930 re-creation of a nineteenth-century stenciled wall for the nation's first law school, Tapping Reeve's Law School in Litchfield, Connecticut. The pattern originates from one in the Doctor Daniel Sheldon House of 1830.

BELOW
This stenciling masterpiece in the Joshua Eaton House in Bradford, Vermont, was painted by Moses Eaton, c. 1824.

The itinerant artist Rufus Porter painted many murals in New England during the early 1800s. These details and one side of a wall are from his parlor frescoes, enhanced with stenciling, that he created for the Doctor Moses Mason House in Bethel, Maine.

Massachusetts, were executed on dry plaster and show his unusual, "scientific" approach to creating perspective and depth of field. The same kind of stencil treatment can be observed in Doctor Moses Mason's house in Bethel, Maine.

In post-Revolutionary America, a surprisingly large number of homeowners from all socioeconomic groups chose intricate stenciled designs for wall decoration. Although stenciled walls were cheaper and more sanitary than those covered with paper, the most compelling reason for widespread use was that they were considered far more stylish than impersonal mass-produced wallpaper. Stencil artists like Porter, Moses, and others freely borrowed wallpaper motifs. In fact, Porter seems to have been inspired by the celebrated French wallpaper mural designer Joseph Dufour, but he could decorate a wall faster and a lot cheaper than it would have cost to install pricey imported wallpapers.

Many families kept their stenciled walls for years, but as fashions evolved and tastes changed, some were painted or papered over. Time took its toll on plaster, which cracked and chipped. Old houses fell into disrepair, changed hands, and

beautiful stencils were lost. Increasingly affordable after the Industrial Revolution, successive generations of wallpaper covered over stenciled walls—hiding some, obliterating some, and preserving others. For an owner of an old house, the discovery of early stenciled walls (or even a fragment of one) offers a wondrous glimmer into the past.

Stenciling in the Victorian Era: Louis Comfort Tiffany and Frederic Edwin Church

Making a small comeback in the late 1800s, stenciling in the Victorian era was more elaborate than early American examples. Louis Comfort Tiffany (1848–1933) stenciled designs for Mark Twain's house in Hartford, Connecticut, and the artist Frederic Edwin Church (1826–1900) created a Persian-style marvel at his home Olana, overlooking the Hudson River. Church's fanciful stenciling on the doors, door frames, arches, and walls mingled with Arabic calligraphy. His decorative, Arabesque style is a delightful interpretation of traditional Islamic stencil motifs. "I am obliged to imagine Persian architecture," he wrote, "then embody it on paper and explain it to a lot of mechanics whose idea of architecture is wrapped up in felicitous recollections of a successful bricke [sic.] schoolhouse or a jail. Still I enjoy this being afloat on a vast ocean, paddling along in the dreamy belief that I shall reach the desired port in due time." Olana's stenciled decorations were created like a painting: Church first drew penciled sketches, and then he made color drawings.

Tiffany shared with Church an admiration for Orientalism, especially after a trip to North Africa and the Near East from 1870 to 1871. Church traveled to Europe and the Middle East with his family from 1867 to 1869. The highly decorated walls covered in stylized foliage, geometric patterns, and Arabic calligraphy of the palace-citadel Alhambra in Granada, Spain, greatly impressed both men. The walls are devoid of the human figure, because in Islamic art, the figure is found only in miniatures or limited to private living quarters. At Laurelton Hall, Tiffany's mansion on Long Island, he used painted stencil canvases depicting tall cypress trees, an Islamic motif; his *muqarnas* (three-dimensional Islamic geometric designs) demonstrate a skillful combination of exotic and natural elements. His motifs range from the East Indian lotus and the Mediterranean peony to the Persian opium poppy. The resplendent atmosphere of Laurelton Hall, described by Tiffany's contemporary Clara Brown Lyman as "charming enough by day, but by night a veritable Arabian Night's dream come true . . ."

OPPOSITE
This stenciled roof detail is from Olana, Frederic Edwin Church's majestic Persian-style home overlooking the Hudson River.

OVERLEAF
This medley includes Church's original stenciling, seen throughout the house. His stencil patterns delineate doorways, window frames, and baseboards, using copper and zinc for gold effect, and tin for silver.

143

Elaborate carvings around niches enhance the lobby of the Hotel Gazelle d'Or-Taroudant in the Atlas Mountain region of Morocco. The traditional tadelakt *clay plaster wall and pilasters are decorated with intricate stenciling.*

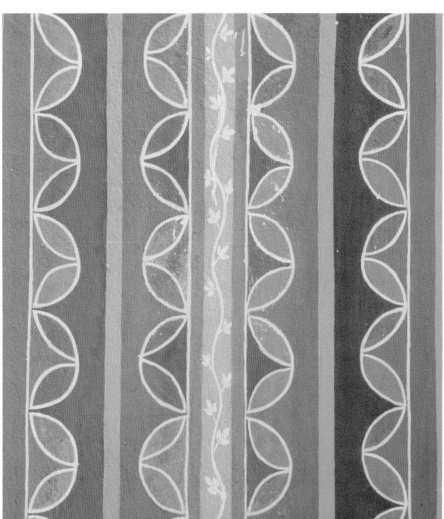

A far cry from Colonial American examples, Church and Tiffany's stenciled creations are infused with exoticism, drawing on influences as diverse as Persia, Turkey, and Morocco, as well as the Alhambra. Arabian stencil ornamentation inspired by Persia can be seen in Morocco today. Interlocking patterns dazzle in sparkling tones of *bleu Majorelle* (cobalt blue) and crimson.

Stenciled Wall Decorations Around the World

The exotic and florid stencils of India, often incorporated in buildings to complement the architecture, date back to ancient times. One traditional technique is the stenciled relief patterns of marble dust and powdered colors seen in the inner sanctuaries of the ancient Vaishnava temples of southern India.

Lively painted walls, joyful colors, and stenciling are part of the rich Mexican culture which harkens back more than a thousand years. As dedicated builders, the Mayans and Aztecs influenced Mexican designs throughout the ages. Blending Spanish taste brought over by the conquistadors in the sixteenth century and the nineteenth-century French design during Emperor Maximilian's reign generated a wealth of wall decorations with a colorful and graphic stenciling tradition. For example, *papel picado*, the Mexican art of creating designs by cutting paper, shows exuberant designs of flowers and lacy scalloped shapes.

Refined stencils in a pale palette grace the walls of an early 1800s residence in San Miguel, Mexico, now home to the design shop Mitu.

148

The Revival of Stenciled Wall Decoration

By the late nineteenth and early twentieth centuries, stenciling didn't have many aficionados. The American interior designer Elsie de Wolfe, in her iconic book *The House in Good Taste* of 1913 had few good words: "The recent vogue of stenciling walls may be objected to . . . though a very narrow and conventional line of stenciling may sometimes be placed just under the picture rail with good effect." One enthusiast, Rudyard Kipling (1865–1936), described "a cozy study" as one "decorated with a dado, a stencil, and cretonne hangings." The British arts and crafts movement, founded by William Morris (1834–1896), kept stenciling alive. Hand-tooled and crafted art and decoration was one of Morris's signature contributions. But the sheer diversity of inexpensive wallpapers curtailed stenciling as an option for wall decoration. This didn't stop Morris, however, from filling his Red House in Bexley Heath (south of London) with wallpaper, tapestry, murals, stenciling, and carvings, all individually finessed, in what he called his "palace of art."

OPPOSITE

A kaleidoscopic geometric stencil pattern colors the wall in Mexico's Hacienda Jaral de Berrio.

ABOVE

A room in the Shiv Niwas Palace Hotel in Udaipur, India, has an intricate pink lotus blossom–border design surrounding the window seat, and the rest of the space is stenciled to echo the exotic furnishings.

BELOW

Enchanting blue-and-white stenciled walls mirror the gorgeous textiles in the Samode Palace, outside of Jaipur, India.

During the art deco era of the 1920s, stencils had a last great hurrah before a long hiatus, but now are back in fashion in many countries. The range of stencil enthusiasts is broad. Even Canada's Inuit community has considered stenciling an important artistic device, which they have reinvigorated since the 1940s. All over the world since the 1970s, stencils are slowly but surely coming back. The desire for handmade, custom-made, personal, and easy patterns began to reappear, making stencils almost as popular as they were in the eighteenth century. Today's translucent stencils, with register marks for alignment of overlaid colors, insure the ease and success of applying even complicated patterns. With a wealth of historic precedent, this decorative technique remains an affordable and attractive way to finish walls. Stencils offer limitless choices to enhance any interior.

RIGHT

A spare, framelike stenciled wall pattern balances the nineteenth-century-style billiard room in the Hacienda Katanchel, outside of Mérida, Mexico.

OPPOSITE

Decorator Thomas Beeton designed this canopied dining room with a fantastical stencil design for a house in Newport, Rhode Island.

OVERLEAF

This sampling of vibrant nineteenth-century wall decoration features stenciled patterns found in Mexico's Hacienda Jaral de Berrio.

OPPOSITE

Joseph Shoskovitch painted the gilded wall and ceiling stenciling in this exotic room of fashion designer Mary McFadden's New York City apartment.

RIGHT

Used for reference, designer Renzo Mongiardino made these stencil samples on glass.

OVERLEAF

A fabric created by Robert Kime inspired the abstract Moroccan stencil pattern in this Los Angeles dining room by interior designer Martyn Lawrence-Bullard.

Decorative painter Karen Lucas looked to Indian motifs to create these wall-stencil designs of stylized natural forms in muted hues of saffron and green.

Nadia Wolinski based these borders of ferns and griffins on neoclassical designs. They enhance a New York City townhouse entrance hall that I designed.

Subtle stencil design is an effective way to accentuate a chair rail.

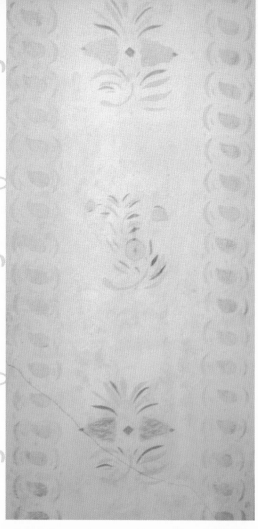

STENCILING ESSENTIALS

COLOR TIPS

- Early American stencilers first painted walls in a gray, raspberry, or yellow ochre wash. They then applied the stencil patterns in rich, vivid colors, such as red, black, green, rust, and ochre.
- Select stencil colors that are dark enough to show the whole design. For example, the early stencilers often painted the fruit part of the pineapple in red because yellow was too pale.
- To make colors appear old, tone them down with raw umber.
- Paint swatches of color on paper first, tape them to the wall, and study the hues in different light.

PAINT TIPS

- Use latex paint, the great modern invention that washes up easily with soap and water.
- Use a flat finish. If you wish to alter a color, mix in acrylic paint. The base is the same. To lighten a color, add white; to darken a color, add black or brown.

RESTORATION TIPS

If you live in an old house, the discovery of stenciling under layers of wallpaper or wallboard is a wonderful surprise. To expose the stenciling and remove the wallpaper, wait for a humid day. Leave the windows open and test the paper to determine if it can be peeled off in unbroken strips. Depending on the size of the room, this task may be accomplished in an afternoon. The stencil pattern may have deteriorated, in which case, restoration will be required, which can be labor-intensive. To start, clean the wall surface with a sponge full of warm water and soap. After removing all the dirt, dry the walls. It will now be easier to evaluate. If repainting is needed, purchase the appropriate latex paints for the type of wall surface, matching the original colors as best as possible. Do touch-ups with a brush. If more extensive restoration is needed, re-create the stencil pattern and try to duplicate the design. It is best to use paint sparingly.

ABOVE: Attributed to the early American stenciler "Stimp," this wall-stencil detail is from the Samuel Clark House in Washington, Connecticut. The apple-green and rose colors stand out on a white rough plaster ground. BELOW: A detail from interior designer James Shearon's floral stenciled wall, which is loosely based on wallpaper. OPPOSITE: A faux twig motif frames the wall of this resort's great room, designed by Jed Johnson in Twin Farms, Vermont. Although painted freehand, it has a stencillike quality.

wallpaper

anger often comes from unexpected places. Sometimes even wallpaper can be deadly, as Oscar Wilde (1854–1900) declared on his deathbed in 1900: "My wallpaper is killing me—one of us must go." Fortunately, wallpaper rarely has had such a negative effect. On the contrary, when appropriately selected, wallpaper has a powerful decorative impact, with the ability to create an ambience and set the tenor of a room. Rich and luxurious, pretty and peaceful, playful and colorful, strong and bold, even educational in some instances, wallpaper makes a personal statement.

Wallpaper dates back farther than most people realize. With many forerunners, it developed in different forms in various cultures. The earliest paper scroll to date is Egyptian, dating back to 2,500 B.C. This rare artifact now in the Louvre consists of the stems of papyrus reeds, which grew in abundance along the banks of the Nile. Made of bark and linen, this early wallpaper was produced for funeral rites and applied to Egyptian tomb walls. Wallpaper, however, seems to have originated in China, where paper was invented in 200 B.C. Alan Victor Sugden and John Ludlam Edmondson's *A History of English Wallpaper* states that the Chinese often lined walls with wood and handmade paper.

Japan acquired the Chinese knowledge of papermaking around 600 A.D. The Japanese also used paper extensively in their houses. Until recently, rice paper was placed over windows to give a diffuse light and stretched over *fusuma*, the dividing screens between rooms. Painted with scenes from nature, such as a landscape, birds, or flowers enhanced with matte-gold accents, *fusuma*, though not exactly wallpaper, is an early use of paper as a decorative wall element.

In the eighth century, papermaking along with wallpaper techniques had spread to the Islamic world. Paper mills were built in Baghdad and Damascus, and the Moors, who invaded Spain in 1150, constructed a mill in North Valencia. A little later, the

This eighteenth-century oil painting of the interior of a wallpaper manufactory interior is in the collection of the Ferens Art Gallery.

French, assisted by the Spanish, built their first mill and later became the most prolific wallpaper makers of the Middle Ages. By 1276, wallpaper began to be produced in Italy. During the next two hundred years, wallpaper manufacturing spread to most European countries, reaching Russia in the sixteenth century, and America and Canada in the seventeenth century.

In both Europe and China, painted wallpapers preceded printed ones. It is recorded that Louis XI paid a painter and illuminator named Jean Bourdichon in 1481 the sum of twenty-four livres for painting fifty rolls of paper in blue with the first line of the eighty-ninth psalm *"Misericordias Domini in Aeternum Cantabo."* (I will sing the mercies of the Lord forever.) Painted and gilded paper trumpeted the French King Louis XII's entry into Lyons in 1507.

During the Renaissance, wallpaper was practical for decorating the court because paper scrolls were easily transported from one castle to another. At this time, wallpaper competed with painted cloth, wall hangings, and tapestries, which were less fragile. However, a paper scroll had the advantage in that it could be produced less expensively in longer lengths. On the beams of the Master's Lodge at Christ's College in Cambridge, England, there is the earliest known fragment of European wallpaper. Dating back to 1509, this attempt to imitate woven material like a tapestry was block printed on a black background, on the verso of paper used for other purposes, a widespread method at the time. Designed to cover the ceilings of churches and palaces, some wallpapers were printed to imitate wood grain or woodcarving. Though deemed the best way to finish a wall or a ceiling at the time, wood paneling was more expensive than wallpaper.

Across the Channel in sixteenth-century France, wallpapers evolved from the endpapers used in bookbinding. The first examples were marbleized patterns printed in small squares, which were eventually glued together into long, rolled-up sheets for easy transportation. The French craftsmen produced *domino*, single sheets of decorated papers, for the middle-class market throughout the first half of the sixteenth century. Founded in 1540, the guild of *Feuilletiers, Cartonniers, Fabricants d'Images et Cartes à Jouer* (master *domino* printers, picture printmakers, and card makers) soon created *papiers de tapisserie*, which were vastly superior in quality. The writer Jacques Savary des Bruslons noted in the *Dictionnaire universel du commerce*:

> A *dominotier* makes a type of tapestry on paper . . . which is used by the poorer classes in Paris to cover the walls of their huts or shops, but at the end of the 17th century [it] was raised to such a peak of perfection and attractiveness that, apart from the large consignments sent to foreign lands and to all the principal cities of the kingdom, there was not a house in Paris, however magnificent, that did not have somewhere, be it in a dressing room or an even more secret place, which was not hung with paper and quite pleasantly decorated.

169

Domino *papers, small sheets of printed patterned paper, cover this trunk. Litchfield Historical Society.*

Wallpaper was fashionable in sophisticated French homes as well as in simpler ones during the end of the seventeenth century. Because the papers reflected local taste and contemporary artistry, they became a stylish replacement for imported *Indiennes* fabric, delightful painted cottons also known as *pintadoes* or *chintes*, which were imported by the British East India Company in large quantities to Europe. When in 1686 Louis XIV prohibited their importation in France, he accidentally gave a boost to the country's wallpaper production.

Floral and Flocked

OPPOSITE

Fortuny-inspired Clarence House wallpaper adds elegance to the walls in the master bedroom of author Annie Kelly and photographer Tim Street-Porter's Los Angeles house.

OVERLEAF

A composite of floral, marbled, and flocked papers. Page 172, top, left: A brown-vine wallpaper fragment taken out of the Whiting House on East Street in Litchfield, Connecticut. Litchfield Historical Society. Right: A marbled wallpaper with stripes. Litchfield Historical Society. Bottom, left: This domino paper, with its distinctive mustard-yellow-and-navy design, served as a decorative book cover. Litchfield Historical Society. Page 173: These examples of flocked papers display a wide range of textured designs. Top: A Manuel Canovas–designed contemporary hot pink, flocked floral wallpaper. Bottom, left: An antique flocked wallpaper fragment. Litchfield Historical Society. Bottom, right: A Romo-designed contemporary flocked wallpaper with green flowers on a brown background.

170

From the 1680s, wallpaper offered an inexpensive alternative to tapestries and leather hangings. An advertisement recording the type of paper available in England in 1702 states: "Imitation of tapestry, flowered Damasks, Sprigs and branches, a wide imitation of Marble . . . Embossed work . . . Flock work." The range of wallpaper designs included the popular flocked paper and colored papers that were enhanced by stenciling. Flocked paper is embossed, which allows a great variety of effects to be produced. Its inspiration came from leather hangings (known as Cordova leather), which were painted with gold or silver foil. Stencils were essential for creating flocked paper—an illustration of how decorative wall techniques are so intertwined. The process involves painting a background color onto paper or canvas, printing or stenciling a design onto it with a slow-drying adhesive, and scattering the flock over the adhesive, which produces a velvetlike pile over the design. Flocking began about 1600 but enjoyed its heyday from 1715 to 1745, when these exceptional papers were exported from France into England. Flocked paper competed with damask, brocade, and cut velvet both in appearance and price. In the 1750s, a high-quality flock paper cost less than half the price of velvet, but even at that price, it was a luxury. The most popular colors were blue, green, and red. By the mid-1750s, flocked papers were flowing the other way across the Channel. The English were producing *papiers bleus d'Angleterre*, fashionable in France, where the refined Marquise de Pompadour (the celebrated mistress of Louis XV) had them installed in her *appartements*. Soon the French manufacturers perfected the technique, advertising their own version as *papiers veloutés*. And once again, the tide turned as the French began exporting this high-quality flock to England.

Though called wallpaper, it was not pasted directly to the wall during most of the seventeenth and eighteenth centuries. Instead, it was adhered to linen, which was then attached to the walls with copper tacks or sometimes secured to wooden battens covering the walls. Twelve or more individual linen sheets were joined together to form a roll, enabling faster printing and more complex designs. These new production techniques for hanging paper required a great deal of skill. As the standard of living in the Western world increased for a large segment of the population, more emphasis was placed on the home. This manifested itself in many ways, including the fashion for wallpapers. By 1712 wallpaper had become so widespread that England began taxing paper that was "painted, printed or stained to serve as hangings."

The Print Room

The fashion for print-room papers started in England with Horace Walpole, who wrote in 1753: "I had cut some prints and glued them to the wall and framed them in the new manner invented by Lord Cardigan, that is with white and black borders printed." This variation of wallpapering, in which engravings were adhered to plain paper, developed in England in the 1760s. Paper stainers made *trompe l'oeil*–painted versions with framed views of temples, ruins, and landscapes. Such rooms became popular all over Europe throughout the eighteenth century, particularly in Germany,

BELOW, LEFT
A repetitive pattern of a castle with pillars on this late nineteenth-century wallpaper. Litchfield Historical Society.

BELOW, MIDDLE
Charlotte and Adam Van Doren's apartment entrance gives the illusion of an historical print room. Adam painted the decorative frames for his print collection.

ABOVE, RIGHT
Depicting a city skyline overlaid with pillars and arches, this wallpaper was probably made for the 1909 Hudson-Fulton Celebration.

OPPOSITE
This wall in the Print Room of Blickling Hall, England, is an artful example of how prints can cover an expansive wall.

Sweden, and Russia. The print room eventually led to the early twentieth-century creation of wallpaper that gives the illusion of walls hung with prints of landscapes, ruins, or other images in frames of all shapes and sizes.

In Sweden, print rooms became chic in the 1780s, after Gustav III decorated a room in the royal palace with engravings by Piranesi. Estates like Almare-Stäket on the outskirts of Stockholm followed suit. The fashionable print room joined forces with an interest in the Gothic, leading to the creation of another popular austere wallpaper, called "pillar and arch," found often in England and America well into the 1770s.

Botanical illustrations,
published by
J. Burmannius in the
eighteenth century,
imaginatively covers
the walls of Carolus
Linnaeus's estate
Hammarby in
Sweden—an early
form of wallpaper.

OPPOSITE
The popular, early
nineteenth-century
"pillar and arch"
wallpaper pattern
covers the walls of a
bedroom at Beauport.

Chinese Wallpaper (Chinoiserie)

At the beginning of the eighteenth century, colored wallpapers dominated, replacing black-and-white ones. Flowered patterns and hand-painted Chinese wallpaper, referred to as *chinoiserie*, became the rage. Imported with great success from the Orient, *chinoiserie* was considered by the elite to be the most stunning and intricate wallpaper.

In the middle of the seventeenth century, travelers, merchants, and missionaries went to the Orient in large numbers and brought back all sorts of *chinoiserie* novelties in many different forms—from lacquer boxes and panels to china. Around 1643 the directors of the powerful British East India Company complained that Indian fabrics were unsuitable for the English market. To ensure the production of desirable goods, they provided patterns to the Indian manufacturers with a precise English idea of how Eastern fabrics should look. Consequently, by the mid-seventeenth century, the English began instructing craftsmen on how to make textiles in the appropriate English "China fashion." Because the Indian weavers were unable to replicate the English designs, they unintentionally created a hybrid style.

Though far removed from classic Chinese tradition, these *chinoiserie* novelties were exported from India to China. In the eighteenth century, Chinese weavers

A Swedish wallpaper of around 1770, with a Chinese-influenced design, decorates the court theater at Drottningholm.

OPPOSITE
This wallpaper fragment with familiar Oriental images—peacocks, pagodas, and cherry trees—is from the Oliver Boardman House on North Street in Litchfield, c. 1916–1925. Litchfield Historical Society.

This Chinese hand-
painted panel with a
flora-and-bird design
was exported by the
Canton school in the
1800s. Carolle Thibaut-
Pomerantz Collection.

OPPOSITE
This detail of a hand-
painted Chinese wallpaper
is from Beauport's China
Trade Sitting Room.

and painters produced fabrics and wallpapers adorned with the traditional Tree of Life design, based on Indian patterns that were derived from English originals and expressions of Europe's vision of Asia. These stylistic developments are an intriguing example of cultural, artistic, and mercantile cross-fertilization. Though printing had been practiced in China for centuries, *chinoiserie* wallpapers were usually painted by hand, in gouache or tempera. The result was charming—a rich and exotic decoration that took Europe by storm.

The first wallpapers imported from the East to Europe and England were regarded merely as inexpensive substitutes for calico or chintz and later banned by an act of Parliament. However, by the early eighteenth century, wallpapers of a superior quality were imported to England and were very costly. Lady Mary Wortley Montagu considered buying some to decorate her Italian villa but abandoned the idea after discovering that damask was less expensive. However, the *chinoiserie* rage remained popular in Italy and throughout Europe during the eighteenth century. Many villas and palaces showcased elaborate Chinese rooms with walls covered in fresco, stucco, lacquer, painted linen, or wallpaper.

Chinoiserie played an important role in the elaborate theatrical spectacles for which Italy is famous. On Augustus the Strong's visit to Venice in 1716, he was greeted by a junk—bristling with parasols, exotic Chinese singers, dancers, and musicians—propelled down the Grand Canal by coolie gondoliers. Firework displays frequently had *chinoiserie* backdrops. *Chinoiserie* wallpapers were deemed suitable for even the most grandiose rooms throughout Europe and often graced with Chinese-style furniture and decorative objects.

These patterns enjoyed success in North America also. In 1738 Thomas Hancock of Boston placed an order for wallpaper with a seller in London, enclosed a pattern he had recently seen, and ordered enough to line two rooms. "Desire you by all means to get mine well done and as cheap as possible, and if they can make it more beautiful by adding more birds flying here and there . . ." The eighteenth-century tastemaker Horace Walpole referred to a drawing room in the "Chinese . . . style that I fancied and I have been executing at Mr Rigby's in Essex; it has large and fine Indian landscapes, with a black fret round them, and round the whole entablature of the room, and all the ground or hanging is of pink paper."

This fanciful wallpaper reached the height of its vogue between 1740 and 1790. Imported in large quantities, *chinoiserie* lined nearly every great house in Europe. The fashion outgrew the supply, and *chinoiserie* fabrics, wallpapers, and objects began to be manufactured in the East for export. This type of *chinoiserie*

Chinoiserie *wallpaper embellishes Caramoor's Apothecary Room.*

183

paper remained popular. The style of hand-painted birds, trees, pagodas, and sometimes Chinese figures in landscapes became known as *chinoiserie*. The paper found its way into manor houses, palaces, and châteaux. It was often applied in panels and could be edged with gilt. European painters copied the Chinese designs, but the French-produced papers were the most sought after.

The most popular Oriental paper imported at this time depicted a tall tree with exotic birds roosting in its branches, perhaps a zigzag fence, a small house, and a group of Chinamen in the foreground. Well-known examples embellish the Chinese drawing room of the Temple Newsam House in Leeds, England. That it is similar to the wallpaper at Caramoor and at the Brighton Pavilion is not surprising, since both papers are believed to have been acquired by the Prince Regent from Crace and Sons in 1802. So Caramoor's papers may come from the same source. The Prince, seeing Lady Hertford at a race meeting, fancied that he was still in love with her, and on September 28, 1806, he paid a morning visit to her home, Temple Newsam House, and presented the young lady's mother with several rolls of wallpaper. Unfortunately, the walls of the house had just been re-covered with

Narrative chinoiserie *wallpaper envelops this powder room.*

Chinoiserie *scenic wallpapers in the entertainment space of an early twentieth-century home function as backdrops to the furnishings. They are each set off in elaborate frames.*

a block-printed paper, and this exotic gift was probably not in keeping with her mother's rather restrained taste. The rolls of wallpaper remained there as a tribute to the prince, who was Lady Hertford's companion until the 1820s.

The fashion for *chinoiserie* among Europeans and the English opened the door to novelty and satisfied a curiosity for the exotic. Its popularity, combined with the steep price and lengthy delivery, prompted English and French manufacturers to develop locally produced papers—a big boost for the wallpaper business. French artisans were first to develop new ways to print larger, more cohesive designs, created by Jean Papillon (1661–1723), and later his son Jean Michel (1698–1776). Many consider Papillon senior to be the true father of wallpaper. The younger Papillon, in his excellent *Traîté historique et pratique*

OPPOSITE
*This grisaille chinoiserie
scenic wallpaper,
designed by Zuber,
serves as an elegant
backdrop for a grand
entrance hallway.*

ABOVE, RIGHT
Chinoiserie *wallpaper
and sculpture define
this Parisian rooftop
dining room designed by
Alberto Pinto.*

BELOW, RIGHT
*This antique chinoiserie
paper graces a dining
room in a Dallas,
Texas home.*

de la gravure en bois (1766) wrote that his father invented *papier peint* (wallpaper), which he called *"tapisserie de papier,"* in 1688. The combination of good design and reasonable prices made *papier peint* an appealing product. In 1795 *Le Journal du Lycée des Arts* gave its blessing: "For appearance, cleanliness, freshness and elegance, these papers are to be preferred to the rich textile of yesteryear." In stark contrast, Edith Wharton (1862–1937) objected to the use of wallpaper on the grounds of both appearance and cleanliness a century later in her book *Decoration of Houses*, published in 1898. "It was well for the future of house-decoration when medical science declared itself against the use of wallpapers. These hangings have in fact little to recommend them. Besides being objectionable on sanitary grounds, they are inferior as wall-decoration to any form of treatment, however simple . . ." Luckily, not every one had the same poor opinion about wallpaper, but it is remarkable how fashion trends impact interior decoration.

European Wallpaper

Led by French manufacturer Jean-Baptiste Réveillon, the late eighteenth and early nineteenth centuries embodied the golden age of French *papier peint*. The French wallpaper historian Henri Clouzot once said of Réveillon, who emerged in the 1770s, that "he gave wallpaper a new language to speak." His firm became a *Manufacture Royale* and produced spectacular papers, particularly in flock. He created quality paper with newly invented, insoluble colors. Previously, only Chinese papers had perfect insolubility, while European colors smudged if the papers were not hung extremely carefully. But the new invention prevented such a disaster.

In 1778 Louis XVI issued a decree that required the length of a wallpaper roll to be about thirty-four feet, making wallpaper a royal affair but not for long. Contemporary newspapers and archives, such as the *Almanach de Paris*, reveal that in 1788 there were forty-eight merchants and manufacturers of *papier peint* in Paris. By the end of the eighteenth century, the wallpaper industry was successful, concentrated in the Faubourg Saint Antoine, the heart of the luxury furnishings district. Réveillon was succeeded by the firm of Jacquemart et Bénard after the French Revolution.

In the German-speaking lands, production was scattered and design was very much under French influence. In fact, the best wallpapers were imported from France until they were banned in 1846. Even a literary giant such as Johann Wolfgang Goethe was fascinated by the effect of interior decoration on the human psyche. In the sixth chapter of his *Theory of Colour*, Goethe argues for a "sensual

Paul Garzotto designed this chinoiserie *dining room—a dramatic composition of red, white, and silver—in Dallas, Texas.*

189

and moral effect of colours." He recommends green wallpapers for rooms in which one spends a lot of time, whereas rooms papered purely in blue may appear larger but in fact come across as empty and cold. The predilection for green wallpaper was dangerous because the green dye was arsenic-based and therefore poisonous. Schiller, Goethe's neighbor in Weimar, apparently had such a wallpaper color, in his study, that poisoned him.

In America wallpaper production started as early as the 1760s. The Boston *News-Letter* reported that "John Rugar produced several Patterns of Paper Hangings made in this Province." In 1755 Edward Ryves, an Irish immigrant, and a partner named Fletcher advertised "A new American Manufactory for paper hangings in

Philadelphia," and claimed they were "the first who have attempted that manufacture on this continent." The information about American wallpaper manufacture increases dramatically after the Revolution. Between 1784 and 1790, almost a dozen paper stainers had established business in Boston and Philadelphia.

In England during the middle of the eighteenth century, John Baptiste Jackson (born in 1700), a pupil of the engraver Elisha Kirkhal, attempted to elevate the art of paper staining with the more durable method of using oil paints for printing. After a visit to Italy, Jackson, who had worked for the younger Papillon in Paris, became interested in Italian Renaissance design. In 1746 he returned to England determined to revive English wallpaper printing, which had taken a beating from the French. But he did not succeed.

French Scenic Wallpaper (Papier Peint Paysage)

This detail from Les Métamorphoses d'Ovide, *c. 1785, a forerunner of scenic wallpaper, originates from the firm of Arthur & Grenard. The grisaille scenes are from Ovid, while the lunettes are based on Boucher's* Four Seasons. *Carolle Thibaut-Pomerantz Collection*

OPPOSITE

The scenic, sepia-toned wallpaper mounted on stretchers in my country dining room have been measured to fit the space. From Campagne Romaine, *it is attributed to the Pignet company, Saint-Genis Laval, c. 1820.*

Scenic wallpaper emerged at the end of the eighteenth century, inspired by panoramic paintings, which reproduced an entire landscape surrounding the viewer. Scenics (as these nonrepeating papers were known), *papier peint–panoramique, papier peint–paysage* (landscape wallpapers), and *tableaux-tentures* (paintings as wall hangings) became popular all over the world. Manufactured exclusively in France, they were sold and commissioned throughout Europe, England, and the United States. Never before had designs been attempted on such a large scale. To cover the walls of a large room without repeating a scene, twenty to thirty lengths were printed, each piece measuring about ten feet high and twenty inches wide. To print such scenes required a great deal of time and energy, with thousands of hand-carved blocks and hundreds of colors. These papers were remarkable not only because of their large scale and complicated overall compositions but also because of intricate, refined touches and attention to even the smallest details. Such rendering required incredible skill and technique because each element had to be built up by superimposing one atop another using flat, opaque colors printed

from woodblocks. The task of carving hundreds—and often close to a thousand woodblocks—was a formidable undertaking. Once the blocks had been cut, a scene was kept in production (as a book is kept in print) for many years. Aside from the challenge and expense of making the blocks, the color combination had to be established, the ground had to be prepared, the sequence of the blocks had to be worked out, as did the drying time in between each impression, before the color could be added. The results were spectacular—at once realistic and yet with the illusion of a large sense of space. These papers were well received, as people felt that they were buying "art."

Two firms dominated the field—the Zuber Company in Rixheim and Dufour in Mâcon and Paris—producing the largest quantity and the most famous *panoramiques*. The Zuber firm, which Jean père turned over to his sons in 1835, created at least twenty-five *panoramiques* during the nineteenth century. Views of faraway lands, with close attention to topographical or architectural details, were their

OPPOSITE

Zuber's Décor Chinois, a type of paper customarily used in formal dining rooms during the early twentieth century, covers Beauport's Belfry Chamber Bedroom.

Designed by Annie Kelly, the dining room in this Los Angeles house is enveloped in Zuber's Isola Bella wallpaper, which is hung above an off-white chair rail.

OPPOSITE

Part of an exotic panoramique, *these two wallpaper panels are from Joseph Dufour's* Les Vues du Bosphore, *c. 1812. Carolle Thibaut-Pomerantz Collection.*

This extraordinary panoramique Bataille d'Austerlitz *(The Victory of Military Strategy) of 1827–29 illustrates Napoleon's greatest victory in a series of scenes. It is attributed to Jourdan & Villar. Carolle Thibaut-Pomerantz Collection.*

hallmark. According to the archives of the Zuber Company, prints, engravings, or etchings inspired many of their papers. Following the successful *Les Vues de Suisse* (Views of Switzerland), Zuber, by 1835, had brought out *Les Vues d'Inde* (Views of India), 1807; *Les Vues d'Italie* (Views of Italy), 1818; *Les Vues d'Ecosse* (Views of Scotland), 1827; *Vues de la Grèce Moderne* (Views of Modern Greece or The Greek Battles), 1827; *Le Brésil* (Views of Brazil), 1829; and *Les Vues de l'Amérique du Nord* (Views of North America), 1834–1836. This final paper of North America became well known when Jacqueline Kennedy had a set installed in the White House during the 1960s. In 1852 Zuber took advantage of a nationalist wave in the United States and republished a previous paper *Views of North America* as *The War of American Independence*. Turning peaceful scenes into battlefields, he substituted the foreground figures, so the Boston Harbor became the Boston Tea Party.

In contrast, Joseph Dufour's (1754–1827) wallpapers were less exotic, showing enthusiasm for the Empire style of the time with more classical forms. Dufour started the company Dufour Frères & Co. in Mâcon, and then moved to Paris in 1806. In the Exhibition of 1819 he received a silver medal for the quality of his papers with the comments:

Considered a precursor of scenic wallpapers, the Arcadian-like Le Jardin Anglais *(also known as* Jardins de Bagatelle*) was designed by Pierre-Antoine Mongin and woodblock printed by Joseph Dufour in 1804. Carolle Thibaut-Pomerantz Collection.*

C'est au chef de cette maison importante (Dufour) que nous devons les premiers paysages camaïeux et coloriés. Ses paysages historiques, ses draperies et notamment ses tentures, ne le cèdent point, en beauté, aux plus riches tentures de soie. Tous les produits de cette belle manufacture démontrent que M. Dufour a la connaissance la plus profonde d'un art qui lui est aujourd'hui si redevable.

(We owe to the director of this important wallpaper company the first colored landscapes. His historic landscapes, drapery, and hangings are as beautiful as the richest silks. All these creations show that Mr. Dufour has a deep knowledge of an art for which we are so grateful.)

His many papers, beautifully printed, remained in production until 1860. Renamed Dufour et Leroy in 1820, the firm produced their most decorative papers during this period. They include groups of antique sculpture in grisaille; some illustrations of well-known literature (*Don Quixote* and *El Cid*); and also views of Venice, London, Paris, the Bay of Naples, and Constantinople. Depicting exquisite architectural settings and the buildings of these historically rich places, Dufour's

company brochure stated that educational motives had inspired him to undertake the production of such papers.

These scenic papers allowed the occupants and guests alike to dream-travel to the paradise of their choice. They sometimes provided a history lesson similar to historical paintings and frescoes. Finally, this type of wallpaper was considered so sophisticated that it was elevated to the status of "art." The admiration and respect it garnered led to display in many international exhibitions—a testament to its importance and lasting value.

Stripes, Dots, and Plaids

During the eighteenth century in England, geometric forms, such as stripes, plaids, and dots, were favored for wallpaper. Earlier, papers with simple patterns appeared as endpapers in books and were used to line boxes, chests, and trunks. Relatively inexpensive to produce because it was printed in one color, this paper required less

The Prussian architect Karl Friedrich Schinkel designed the surprisingly simple Tent Room in the Charlottenhof Palace in Potsdam, Germany. Documented in this c. 1830 watercolor, this room, based on the Roman Caesar's tent, is clad in blue-and-white striped wallpaper, which covers both the ceiling and walls. The window and bed treatments continue the design.

skill in handling the printing blocks. Equally popular in three countries—France, England, and America—it is often hard to identify from where these papers emanated. The device for applying colored stripes was among the first mechanized improvement in the traditional methods of creating wallpapers, making them relatively affordable. The striped wallpaper reminiscent of a military campaign insignia became a favorite in Napoleonic France as well as in England. Not only did stripes paper the wall, but they also were extended to the ceilings—a practice that spread throughout Europe. Outstanding examples of these papers are attributed to the German architect Karl Friedrich Schinkel. During the early twentieth century, American architect Gustav Stickley embraced striped wallpaper; he discussed its beauty in his monthly publication *The Craftsman*. Graphic stripes in addition to plaids and dots became a standard offering of the wallpaper trade that continues to this day.

ABOVE, LEFT

Stripes energize any room, as with the walls of this Catherine Grenier– designed room in Cadiz, Spain, which are covered in horizontal-striped wallpaper by Osborne and Little.

ABOVE, RIGHT

Playful, vinyl-dot wallpaper by Vescom enhances a hallway designed by Catherine Grenier in Cadiz, Spain.

ABOVE, LEFT
Bold red-striped wallpaper adds pizzazz to a sitting room.

BELOW, LEFT
My son's bedroom has a masculine feel due to this crisp, bold green-striped wallpaper, carefully mounted in an alcovelike space to create a striking pattern.

OPPOSITE
Classic plaid transfers well to wallpaper, as in this bedroom where French interior designer Jean-Louis Denoit has created a cozy niche in the bed alcove.

Toile de Jouy

Interior decorator Martyn Lawrence-Bullard designed this sophisticated black-and-white toile de Jouy bathroom for a Los Angeles house.

OPPOSITE

My brown-and-off-white toile de Jouy bedroom ensemble in Connecticut is a peaceful haven.

Once upon a time a king, a queen, and their courtiers sported novel fabrics for their waistcoats and gowns to be worn in the palaces. By the 1780s, fickle fashion favored small vignettes depicting allegorical scenes, romanticized rustic courtships in the style of the painters Watteau and Fragonard, as well as contemporary events. These scenes printed on cotton in single colors—either red, in the manner of *sanguine* (red chalk drawing), or blue, in imitation of the *chinoiserie* patterns of blue-and-white china—became immensely popular by the late eighteenth century for both clothing and furnishings. Louis XVI and his queen, Marie Antoinette, loved it and so did the rulers that followed. Universally known as "toile de Jouy" after the town

of origin, these cotton toiles popularized a textile genre that is still around. Its success was based on proximity to the Versailles factory, which enabled courtiers to visit frequently, and a keen eye for changing tastes with an ability to implement new techniques to industrialize production. Toile patterns in wallpaper soon followed.

The simple color scheme of toile—usually a single color, such as blue, red, green, or black, on a white background—gave it a bold look. Another attraction was its picture-book quality, documenting the achievements, pleasures, and preoccupations of the era. In addition to the well-known depictions of the four seasons, elements, corners of the world, the Holy sacraments, and famous monuments, the cottons were decorated with fashionable *chinoiserie*, copies of recently discovered Pompeii paintings, subjects from literature such as La Fontaine's *Fables*, mythology, and history. Current events provided the most edifying examples: nobles savages abounded, as did images of a young America honoring France.

OPPOSITE

This blue-and-white toile de Jouy wallpapered bathroom befits its summery locale in Southampton, New York.

ABOVE, RIGHT

The blue-and-white striped bed canopies, boldly trimmed in orange, handsomely set off the toile de Jouy wallpaper in this Jean-Louis Denoit–designed bedroom.

BELOW, RIGHT

The purple-and-black toile de Jouy master bedroom that I designed in a New York City townhouse creates a calm retreat from urban chaos.

207

Borders and Friezes

A composite of borders.
Above: A detail of a rose
border plucked from a
pastoral scene wallpaper.
Middle: This wallpaper
features a pineapple-
topped column, a symbol
of hospitality, with
a neoclassical-style
leaf border. Below:
This early nineteenth-
century wallpaper
border fragment features
the guilloche motif, a
repetitive pattern of two
curved interlacing bands
used in neoclassical
architecture. This
attractive design was
revived during the
Federal period. Litchfield
Historical Society.

OVERLEAF
A collection of borders
and friezes. Page 210,
top: A Greek key and
blue swag border by
Clarence House. Bottom:
A black-and-brown
border by Cowtan &
Tout is festooned with
repetitive diamond and
other stylized motifs.
Page 211, top: A gold
rosette-and-flower border
by Scalamandre. Middle,
left: A brown-and-white
featherlike design rests
atop blues and greens to
form a pleasing border
design. Middle, right: A
Classical Revival border
in cheerful gold, blue,
and orange. Bottom: A
green-and-white rope
border, another Classical
Revival design.

208

Almost as old as wallpaper itself, borders originally hid the tacks that held the paper in position. Prominent by the late 1700s, wallpaper borders could visually alter a room's proportions. Popular border designs featured floral and architectural friezes. Many were printed to look like a cornice and were hung where the wall and ceiling joined to add importance and grandeur to a room. Often they outlined doors and windows or architectural details, such as a fireplace, doors, or a baseboard, within the room. Architectural fakery became a major part of the wallpaper stock-in-trade. These designs were produced mainly in France and exported throughout Europe and America—paper columns, coffered ceilings, friezes imitating carved moldings, as well as dados that looked like paneling. Pseudo-balustrades were favored for below the chair rail on walls covered with scenic paper.

By the beginning of the 1800s, it was fashionable to divide the wall into three parts—dado, filler, and frieze. Often the borders running along the top were a mirror image of those on the bottom. Friezes borrowing carved elements from classical architecture along with some imitation drapery swags became the rage. Swag borders were everywhere—hung above simple repeating patterns and stripes and above landscape scenes. Swag borders paired with wallpaper substituted for expensive draped fabric. English writer John Claudius Loudon (1783–1843), in his *Encyclopedia of Cottage, Farm and Villa Architecture and Furniture* of 1833 encouraged the use of borders with wallpaper: "The side walls of a room equally ornamented in every part . . . by a rich paper would be intolerable were it not for the contrast produced by the plain ceiling and by the border with which the paper is finished under the cornice at top and above the base or surbase below."

When "wallpaper" appeared in nineteenth-century advertisements, it was usually accompanied by the word "borders." However, not everyone loved friezes and borders. The American decorator Elsie de Wolfe, in her book *The House in Good Taste*, firmly stated: "Those dreadful friezes . . . perpetuated by certain wallpaper designers are very bad form and should never be used. Indeed, the very principle of the ordinary paper frieze is bad: it darkens the upper wall unpleasantly." I disagree with this claim. Friezes and borders can be beautiful in the right place. As the cost of fabrics and millwork run much higher, they are an affordable alternative, especially for those who prefer not to have the allover pattern of wallpaper.

In the Victorian era, it was Britain's turn to innovate. The repeal of wallpaper taxation in 1836 and a breakthrough in production encouraged English designers

212

to produce their own complex designs. A calico-printing firm, Potters of Darwen in Lancashire, England, created a printing machine for wallpaper, patented in 1839. As wallpaper production increased, prices dropped, and more people could buy it for their homes. Applying wallpaper became easier because it could now be placed directly on plaster. A variety of patterns were designed, some even suitable for a child's nursery. The front hall of a Victorian house sometimes boasted bright-colored paint and wallpaper embellished with scrolls and flowers.

Though largely initiated in England, the industrialization of wallpaper caused the British to react to the limits imposed by mechanization. By the late 1800s, British designers such as William Morris and Owen Jones (author of *The Grammar of Ornament*, 1856) began to rebel against the excesses of the mid-century. They wanted to restore good taste and re-establish quality workmanship. Morris, for example, insisted on the purest colors and techniques; his influence is evident in the hundreds of mass-produced papers manufactured from the 1880s until the end of the century. The irony is that when Morris started Morris, Faulkner & Co., around 1861, he wrote that he did not like wallpaper. He considered it an inferior replacement for the handiwork of the rich tapestries he loved. As a child, Morris saw a tapestry hanging in Queen Elizabeth's lodge in Epping Forest—"a room hung with faded greenery" that became imprinted on his imagination. Tapestries embodied the artistic conflict at the center of Morris's endeavors and of the Arts and Crafts movement itself. They were labor-intensive and beyond the means of the working classes for whom he aspired to design them. Morris initially produced wallpapers with botanicals he remembered from his days in Epping Forest and the gardens at his beloved Red House. Unfortunately, few of his early designs sold well, so it was years before he returned to wallpaper.

However, by 1875 Morris revisited wallpaper and produced about nineteen new designs within the next few years; some of the patterns for wallpaper and textiles have become enduring classics. The Pre-Raphaelite designs were suggestive of medieval and oriental themes—dense, elongated patterns drawn from nature. The vogue for such repetitive patterns—especially flowers—persisted in both England and France throughout the

nineteenth century. Many of these designs derived from Morris's passion for the romantic past of noble knights and wistful princesses.

The art nouveau style of Continental Europe introduced papers with more elegant and refined flowers—daturas, irises, and freesias—as well as plain-colored papers with scenic friezes. Artists such as Alfonso Mucha (1869–1939) and Hector Guimard (1867–1942) designed large figurative or abstract panels. Josef Hoffmann (1870–1956), a founder of the Wiener Werkstätte and a favorite of Elsie de Wolfe, created strong black-and-white patterned papers, influenced by Charles Rennie Mackintosh, a prominent figure in the international art nouveau movement.

In 1907 Hermann Muthesius formed the first Deutscher Werkbund, a German association of artists, architects, and designers whose aim was to integrate traditional craft and mass production. Between 1910 and 1917, many Werkbunds were established in Austria, Switzerland, and Sweden. Several outstanding wallpaper designers were connected to the Werkbunds. Morris, the founder of the English Arts and Crafts movement, particularly inspired them. Notable among them are Georges Lemmen (1865–1916), whose work integrates elements of art nouveau and art deco; Henry van de Velde (1863–1957) whose highly detailed designs are linear in nature; and Walter Leistikow (1865–1908), whose art nouveau designs were tempered by the restraint of the Japanese style. Nineteen-nineteen saw the founding of the Bauhaus in Weimar—an important movement for the decorative arts. Unfortunately, wallpaper no longer had a place in this more constrained, industrial environment.

Simultaneously, in France there was a reaction to the floral patterns of the art nouveau movement and the functional designs of modernism. A new, sophisticated style known as art deco appeared. Leading designer Emile-Jacques Ruhlmann epitomized the glamour of this look. By the 1920s, futurist and cubist designs arrived on the market, making both modern and traditional patterns available. A group of designers created unusual and beautiful wallpapers once again. The bright colors of this new French style brim with *joie de vivre*, the polar opposite of Germany's Bauhaus style. In the 1930s, silkscreen printing was used for wallpaper production as it still is today. Vinyl wallpaper in 1947 and the pre-pasted papers of the 1950s burst with innovation. Around the same period, wallpaper firms in Europe and America commissioned well-known artists including Henri Matisse, Joan Miró, Alexander Calder, and Andy Warhol, to design high-end wallpapers. Once again fine artists created wallpapers. Available to the general public, these special designs were publicized in lifestyle magazines and glamorized the image of old-fashioned wallpaper.

A sampling of early twentieth-century wallpapers. Top, left: An Emile-Jacques Ruhlmann–designed wallpaper of 1912, which was printed by Desfossé & Karth in 1918–23. Several examples of art deco wallpapers designed by J. Granil in 1928–30. Top, middle: This panel depicts jazzy, abstract orange-yellow flowers. Top, right: A design of large, floating abstract leaf patterns in vibrant colors stands out against a muted background. Bottom, left: A composition of abstract roses in a variety of reds. Bottom, middle: A tightly designed, overall pattern of abstract flowers in blue and beige. Bottom, right: Biomorphic flowers and leaves are delicately linked by brown vines. Carolle Thibaut-Pomerantz Collection.

This bohemian wallpaper enlivens a Catherine Grenier–designed kitchen in Madrid.

OPPOSITE

Interior designer Thomas Beeton commissioned this frescoed chinoiserie wall by Dana Westring for a Los Angeles bathroom. This effect can be achieved with chinoiserie-style wallpaper, an affordable alternative.

With the emergence of post–World War II prosperity, no wallpaper style dominated. The spectrum of choices—from historic paper to antique remnants—accommodated personal tastes and needs. Wallpaper can give character to a simple room or be a whimsical solution. It can last a hundred years and still look good. It is a clever camouflage for problematic spaces and a solution to cover cracks. As Elsie de Wolfe says in *The House in Good Taste*: "If your walls are faulty, you must resort to wallpapers . . . Properly selected wallpapers are not to be despised. . . . Among the most enchanting of the new papers are the black-and-white ones, fantastic Chinese designs and startling Austrian patterns." Go ahead, paper your walls, but keep in mind the unique character of each room.

LEFT

A modern interpretation of the print room—one of several paintings on canvas by Elizabeth Thompson that hang above a couch in my New York City apartment living room—makes for witty and chic decoration.

OPPOSITE

Classically inspired wallpaper in my contemporary billiard room lends instant age to a new structure.

WALLPAPER ESSENTIALS

Wallpaper is ideal for many rooms. It is perfect for small hallways and bathrooms. If the space is limited and dark, do not hesitate to be dramatic. Use bold stripes, big patterns, and textured paper such as flock.

Wallpaper can be cheery in bedrooms, especially when used together with fabrics that extend the pattern and coordinate with curtains or bedcovers. This decorative treatment will make a large room feel cozy. In a bedroom, you need to tread more carefully, so the walls aren't claustrophobic. The light and architecture of a room need to be considered. Wallpaper can disguise an irregular-shaped room. Use lighter colors and soft designs in a bedroom with southern exposure. To add some height to a room, use vertical stripes enhanced with white. Chinese wallpaper, or those with scenic motifs, are good choices for a dining room. Toile de Jouy paper looks best when coordinated with fabrics for furniture, draperies, and bed treatments. These papers look dramatic in an entranceway, provided the space is large enough. Steer clear of busy patterns and jarring colors as they are overwhelming, especially in a dining room. The choices are limitless, but editing is important. Discriminate in your use of patterns.

MAINTENANCE

- Monitor the temperature and the humidity of a wall-papered room. Be aware that strong sunlight can fade a paper, and moisture encourages mold and insects. If your wallpaper is lifting, make sure insects have not burrowed underneath. Also check for color flaking, which is caused by humidity. Take care of such conditions immediately to avoid further damage.
- When wallpapering a sunny room, make sure that windows are ultraviolet filtered and have blinds.
- Polishes, cleaning fluids, and fungicidal agents must be kept away from wallpaper.
- Do not push furniture against wallpaper as you may cause tearing or abrasion.

REMOVAL

- A likely place to find old wallpaper is under wood-work. Make a record of everything before tampering with it. Old wallpaper is brittle, so consult a professional. The bottom paper can frequently be eased off in large sheets by inserting a flat-bladed knife between the plaster and the paper.
- Do not roll old wallpaper as it will crack. Keep it flat.
- Small fragments can be treated like drawings. Mount them on acid-free cardboard before framing.
- If presented with a "paper sandwich" (many layers stuck together), steam them apart.

ABOVE: A detail of a purple, coral-patterned Clarence House wallpaper from my pool house bathroom. LEFT: A detail of a blue, green, and pink scallop-patterned Brunschwig and Fils wallpaper brings to mind antique Florentine paper. OPPOSITE: Depicting tropical wildlife, this c. 1890 wallpaper was popular at the turn of the twentieth century. Litchfield Historical Society.

acknowledgments

Creating this book has been an enormous pleasure. Wall decoration in all its forms has long been a favorite subject of mine. The exquisite photographs of inspiring decorative treatments are primarily the work of Tim Street-Porter, Pieter Estersohn, Brian Van den Brink, and Ingalill Snitt. Fine examples have also been secured from photography archives and other sources around the world. In particular, Edward Whitley at the Bridgeman Art Library has been a godsend, and Merceds Santos-Miller of Caramoor deserves a very special nod.

This project is also a tribute to friends, family, clients, and colleagues who have always been supportive. I wish to thank Barbara Bradbury-Pape, Philip Delves Broughton, Terry Campion, Nancy Chute, Suzy Coolidge, Bertrand de Courville, David Duncan, John Hall, Douglas Hyland, Annie Kelly, Fran Kiernan, Wolfram Koppe, Sheila Kotur, Karen Lucas, Christine McCarty, Sue Ann Marolda, Beverly Mosh, Joseph Montebello, Nabil Nahas, Bertrand Rondot, Stephanie Dello Russo, Dana and Edwin Schulman, Robert Speed, Peggy Tagliarino, Elizabeth Thompson, Carolle Thibaut-Pomerantz, Adam and Charlotte Van Doren, Stanley Weissman, Christine Wiesner, and Nadia Wolinski. My sister Catherine Grenier and brother-in-law Gabriel Burgio were extremely helpful as was their friend Orazio Arezzo, who has made me want to tour Sicily because of his dreamy palace images.

Beatrix de Guitaut graciously put me in touch with the owners of the best painted walls of the French countryside. Stephen Butkus at the Gunn Memorial Museum in Washington, Connecticut, and Cathy Field at the Litchfield Historical Society opened their archives and allowed me to share their remarkable collections. And thank you to Renate and Thomas McKnight for his beautiful work and her photographs—a great team effort! And, I heap high praise upon the owners and designers whose work is illustrated in these pages.

I send a most profound thank you to my friend Angeline Goreau, who can always be counted upon for help and guidance. Many thanks also to the diligent work of my delightful editor Sandy Gilbert. She is a real friend and a terrific, thoughtful editor, who miraculously manages to make the most grueling part of the book fun! I would also like to thank the talented behind-the-scenes Hilary Ney.

With the joy of publishing yet another Rizzoli book, my deepest gratitude goes to Charles Miers for his support and insightful advice. I thank Jessica Napp for her constant support along with the rest of the Rizzoli family. I wish to thank especially Susi Oberhelman for being such a team player and for her talented graphic design—the final piece of the puzzle and a magnificent one.

Finally, I thank my husband Sean for his support and my children—Aymar, Cameron, and Valentina—who have been most helpful and are happy to see this new project finished. Until the next one!

PHOTO CREDITS

Orazio Arezzo: 24, 43 (below)

Antoine Bootz: 157

Bridgeman Art Library: 18, 21, 26, 27, 38, 39, 43 (above), 44, 45, 48, 50, 54, 55, 66, 70, 71, 92, 95, 98, 100, 118, 125, 126, 168, 175, 190 (left), 200, 212

Courtesy of Caramoor (photographs by Gabe Palacio), 99, 107, 132

Courtesy of Château d'Epoisses, Bourgogne, France: 94

Courtesy of Château de Vaulserre, Isere, France: 35

Pieter Estersohn: 2, 6, 11, 16, 22, 23, 25, 28, 30, 31, 33, 34, 42, 56, 57, 60, 61, 72, 83, 85, 86, 87, 88, 91, 101, 102, 103, 110, 111, 114, 115, 121, 127, 128, 129, 146, 147, 151, 156, 162 (below), 163, 166, 184, 185, 186, 187, 188, 206, front cover

Courtesy of Catherine Grenier: 201, 216

Courtesy of the Gunn Memorial Museum, Washington, Connecticut: 52, 109, 133, 137, 162, 174 (right)

Courtesy of Kungl.Hovstaterna/Stockholm, Sweden (photographs by Alexis Daflos): 37, 51

Courtesy of Karen Lucas: 160

Renate McKnight: pages 14, 15

Ingalill Snitt: 68, 108, 131, 176, 178

Tim Street-Porter: 1, 4-5, 9, 10, 12, 40, 41, 46, 47, 53, 58, 59, 62, 64, 73, 75, 76, 77, 78, 79, 81, 82, 84, 96, 97, 104, 105, 112-113, 116, 130, 134, 135, 138, 142, 144, 145, 149, 150, 152, 153, 154, 155, 158, 159, 161, 164, 169, 171, 172, 173, 174 (left and middle), 177, 179, 181, 182, 190 (right), 193, 194, 195, 202, 203, 204, 205, 207, 209, 210, 211, 213, 217, 218, 219, 220, 221, 222, endpapers, author photograph

Courtesy of Carolle Thibaut-Pomerantz Collection: 180, 191, 192, 196, 197, 198-199, 214

Brian Van den Brink: 139, 140, 141

Note: Every effort has been made by the publisher to credit the rights holders and photographers of the images included in this book. Any inadvertent omissions will be corrected in future editions.

First published in the United States of America in 2011
by Rizzoli International Publications, Inc. • 300 Park Avenue South • New York, New York 10010 • www.rizzoliusa.com

Text copyright © 2011 Florence de Dampierre

All rights reserved. No part of this publication may be reproduced, stored in a retrieval system, or transmitted in any form or by any means, electronic, mechanical, photocopying, recording, or otherwise, without prior consent of the publisher.

2011 2012 2013 2014 / 10 9 8 7 6 5 4 3 2 1

Printed in China
ISBN-13: 978-0-8478-3594-2

Library of Congress Control Number: 2010940993

Project Editor: Sandra Gilbert • Designer: Susi Oberhelman, SVO Graphic Design

PAGE 1: *This detail of the Chinese-style Zuber wallpaper, Décor chinois, adorns the guest bedroom at Beauport, the summer house of collector Henry Davis Sleeper. During the early twentieth century, such wallpaper was typical of formal dining rooms.*

PAGE 2: *The frescoes in the former seventeenth-century ballroom of the Villa Antinori delle Rose, now owned by the Ferragamo family, are enhanced with classical architecture and decoration in the style of Piranesi. A vignette of sofas and ottomans upholstered in blue silk velvet and a 1970s travertine cocktail table add a modern touch.*

PAGES 4–5: *This wall mural of flowering vines is a simplified version of an eighteenth-century chinoiserie wallpaper in Drottningholm Palace, Stockholm. New York interior decorator Tim Whealon designed this Park Avenue apartment entry.*

PAGE 222: *A wallpaper collage made from Le Figaro newspaper cuttings cleverly enhances a cozy corner in Beauport.*

FRONT ENDPAPERS:
A detail from the "pillar and arch" wallpaper popularized in the early nineteenth century graces a bedroom at Beauport.

Toile de Jouy wallpaper is joyous, especially in purple and black.

This view of exotic flora and fauna in shades of blue and white is from a hand-painted eighteenth-century chinoiserie wallpaper in Caramoor's dining room.

BACK ENDPAPERS:
This detail is from a chinoiserie hand-painted wallpaper that embellishes the walls of Caramoor's Apothecary Room.

Adam Van Doren's unexpected contemporary Print Room creation makes for a dramatic entrance to his New York City apartment.

This detail of a stenciled wall (now in Mitu, a lovely home furnishings shop) originally comes from an early 1800s house in San Miguel, Mexico.